WALKING IN A MINEFIELD

A SOJOURNER'S GUIDE TO OVERCOMING LIFE'S OBSTACLES

Del Bates

CrossLink Publishing
Rapid City, SD

CrossLink Publishing
1601 Mt. Rushmore Rd, STE 3288
Rapid City, SD 57702

Ordering Information:
Quantity sales. Special discounts are available on quantity purchases by corporations, associations, and others. For details, contact the "Special Sales Department" at the address above.

Walking in a Minefield/Bates —1st ed.

ISBN 978-1-63357-322-2

Library of Congress Control Number: 2020936166

First edition: 10 9 8 7 6 5 4 3 2 1

Published in association with Cyle Young of the Hartline Literary Agency, LLC.

Praise for *Walking in a Minefield*

It has been my joy and pleasure to know Del Bates for several years. She is a woman of faith in God and His power. Del has written a book of warfare and winning in, "Walking In A Minefield." It's an imperative weapon of our warfare - right up there next to God's precious Word - for winning our battle with our enemy. It will bless and change your life!

—Rev. Joyce Ostendarp, West Palm Beach, Florida

Del has written a Spiritual Warfare Handbook that every Christian needs to own, study, and share. From admitting that we serve a real God, but we also oppose a real enemy, to understanding the importance of intercessory prayer, to learning how to avert the plans of the enemy—this book is packed with powerful, applicable information. This spiritually mature author shares her knowledge in a real, raw and practical way through anecdotes and biblical backing. This is a must read!

—Michelle Medlock Adams, Award-winning, Best-selling Author of more than 90 books including "Platinum Faith" (Abingdon Press)

Not all books, not even good books come as a voice from above, but this one does. It does because its author, Del Bates, listens to the voice of the spirit which breathes throughout her newest book, Walking In A Minefield.

—Bishop, Evangelist, Frank Seamster

Every church needs spiritual mothers and fathers to teach the younger spiritual men and women, by example and interaction, what it looks like to trust God and walk according to His Word. Del Bates is a spiritual mother in our fellowship. She has been called to intercede and speak into the lives of the hurting, the wounded and the downtrodden. She takes spiritual warfare very seriously and ministers the Word of God in a way that edifies the body of Christ. I am blessed to be her pastor and friend.
—Pastor Greg Sempsrott, Senior Pastor Vero Bible Fellowship, Vero Beach Florida

Behind the scene of broken homes, drug abuse, an X-rated society, murder and war, there's an Evil Spiritual Reality! An Enemy who's defeated the strongest - Samson, the wisest - Solomon, and a man after God's own heart - David. His very name calls forth our worst nightmares - Satan! In "Walking in a Minefield," Del Bates masterfully articulates the Weapons and Strategies for us to be Victors in Christ Jesus rather than Victims in this conflict of the ages. Readers will not only discover how to be, "more than conquerors" through God's Word and Spirit, but experience new dimensions of His love, joy and peace!
—Dr. Philip Krist, D. Min., Lead Pastor of Lakeside Assembly of God

In the many years that Del Bates has been in the ministry, she has walked through numerous trials and tribulations. She with and through the power of the Holy Spirit has purposed to write this book on minefields. What a powerful undertaking because the enemy set all kinds of bombs in her way. Del refused to allow the enemy to stop her from bringing forth this timely message.

Now more than ever we have needed someone like Del to give us insight into the minefields and how to overcome them with the power of God's Word. She gives spiritual insight to believers as she shares the battles from her own walk with Lord. Thank you so much for your personal wisdom and insight into the deliverance God has for each of us.

—**Pastor Nancy Hart, New Hope Ministries, Vero Beach, FL**

This is one powerful book. Del drew me in from her opening words. She delves deep into so many questions about spiritual warfare that beckoned to be answered. I'm so glad she took on the battle to write this book. I now feel more armed and ready to face my daily mine fields.

—**Jill Roman Lord, Award winning, Best-selling author of over 20 children books including That Grand Easter Day (Selah Award)**

What at timely book Del has written. Many of us have seen the result of our ignorance in fighting the spiritual war that surrounds us. We didn't "engage" in the fight and became victims of the plans of the enemy. One of our biggest foes is passivity. Del opens our eyes to the reality of the battle and encourages us to engage. Victory is ours if we do!

—**Sherry Anderson, FL State Leader of Aglow International and author of Rising from Defeat, the Overcomer's Handbook.**

To my husband Jon, who has spent many nights

alone as I'd hideaway...to type away.

Thank you for your love, support, and encouragement.

"The gospel is like a caged lion. It does not need to be defended, it simply needs to be let out of its cage."
—Charles Spurgeon, 1878

Contents

FOREWORD

"We're living in a war zone," I told my daughter recently during a phone call.

We were not *really*, but it certainly felt that way. Our bathrooms were under renovation, and one of those bathrooms included a large closet, which meant all our clothes had to be "evacuated" before work could begin. The master bath is also a large room, complete with artwork and furniture. All that had to be evacuated as well. The rest of our home was now strewn with clothes, furniture, items from all the bathroom cabinets and drawers . . .

We were living in chaos. Everywhere we stepped, something was in the way. I dodged shoes and wayward trash cans and the runners the workers had laid so that they didn't track on our carpet. I tripped over rolls of toilet paper (*How did they get there?*). And, in the midst of all of this, I read Del Bates' book, *Walking in a Minefield*, thinking *yep. I get it. I get it.*

The problem with most American Christians is that we have never truly lived in a war zone. Since the mid-1800s, our country has not seen the destruction of brother fighting against brother. We have experienced dust bowls and tornados, hurricanes and earthquakes, out-of-control fires, and most assuredly, the COVID-19 outbreak of 2020. But, other than Pearl Harbor and 9-11, we have not experienced the devastation true war leaves behind in our own backyard. Therefore, we find it difficult, I believe, to understand the battleground we face every day on a spiritual war zone.

Years ago, I visited several of our Civil ar battlefields, including Antietam, where I stood with hands-on hips and declared, "They were sitting ducks. No wonder this was our bloodiest single-day battle to date." The Battle of Antietam left a "river of blood," with 22,717 dead, wounded, or missing. Why? Perhaps that is too complicated to explain, and this is certainly not American History 101, but the bottom line is this: the men on the battlefield were over-exposed—enemy to enemy. The South was outnumbered, and the North experienced a surprise-attack. And, I think, they were just too ill-prepared for what they were about to face.

As Christians, we face a battle such as the one fought at Antietam, and not just one day. Every *single* day, the enemy has one goal: to kill, steal, and destroy us (see John 10:10). As a dear friend of mine once said, "Satan doesn't have many tricks in his bag, but those he has, he knows well how to use."

But we serve a God who is greater than any of those tricks and He has given us the weapons of warfare we need to become victorious in the both the battles and the overall war. In the book you hold in your hand, Del Bates explains it all in such detail, you will feel equipped for whatever Satan pulls out of the bag to use against you. You will understand your role as your fight behind your General. You will read story after story from the Bible as well as from Del's life and the lives of those she knows and loves. And you will be blessed by someone I have known for nearly twenty years . . . someone I have watched live out everything she has written about in these pages. She is a true prayer warrior. Her exterior is lovely to behold. Her voice is soft and kind. But do not be fooled. When this warrior for Christ goes into fight-mode, she is not to be messed with! She is a true soldier for Christ, and I am blessed beyond measure to call her my friend.

You will be, too.

Eva Marie Everson
Multiple award-winning author & speaker
President, Word Weavers International

PREFACE

Welcome, and thank you for taking a lunge into learning how to avert the bombs of the enemy.

What you hold in your hands today is a compilation of blood, sweat, and years! Gotcha, didn't I? You thought you knew what I was going to say, but as my grandson says, "I tricked you!"

First, it's all about the blood—the *power* we have in the precious blood of Jesus. If you're anything like me and you never understood the power that lives inside us and has trickled down from that cross on Calvary over two thousand years ago, this is definitely for you! That is why I am so glad you picked up this book. I want to help you discover what I've learned so that you can go forth in victory.

And the sweat is the sweat of the many prayers as I've knocked on heaven's door over and over to avert the bombs of the enemy for myself, my family, and others.

And the tears ... no, the *years* ... true-life stories interwoven with Scripture where I and others have decreed and declared the Word of God, and have seen the powerful outcome of God's hand in motion as He saw fit to answer.

As I sat across the table at a Serious Writer Conference with a dear friend, Gloria Penwell Holtlander, our conversation went something like this: "You're writing a book *on what*?" she asked. Then she added, "Oh honey, you know you better find yourself three powerful prayer warriors before you go on."

While Gloria had a sneak preview of what my year ahead would be like, I was oblivious. The day the Lord asked me to write a book on spiritual warfare, I was excited and all in ... until about one week later, when my younger sister called to let me know she had breast cancer.

That was just the beginning. Looking back, I can say the attacks haven't stopped. That is why I know today that Satan is real: because of what he has done and continues to do to derail me from completing this book. (Good luck with that, Satan. I serve a more powerful God!)

And for you, so loved by your heavenly Father, as you are holding this book in your hands I pray for you to be able to learn how to fight the invisible war you face every day. God's love for you is so great, He's provided a way out of whatever it is you're facing today.

Come with me on this journey. Learn to walk in the minefield of life and discover how to avert the plans of the enemy!

Praying Always,

Del

ACKNOWLEDGMENTS

It is so difficult to thank the many people who have encouraged and stood alongside me to make this dream become a reality.

First, I would like to thank my family. My husband, Jon, my children, Michael, Brian, Jennifer, Pete, Pam, and Jen, who never stopped encouraging me that I could do it. Also, my five precious grandchildren, Cesare, Nina, Izabela, Giuliana, and Vincenzo, always asking, "Are you done with *that* book yet ?"

Next, I'd like to thank my four mighty prayer warriors for continuing to pray for me and for their faithfulness to message me whenever the Lord gave them a word. Each one prayed daily in their own way for the wisdom of the Holy Spirit to fill me with His words so that you could be holding this book in your hands today. Thank you, Sandra Castiglione, Marty Fleming, Karen McKay, and Shirley Morgan ... I owe you.

Next, I'd like to thank my agent, Cyle Young with Heartline Literary Agency, for his continued work as an agent to find a home for my manuscript. Keep up the good work Cyle!

Eva Marie Everson, thank you for the heartwarming Foreword to this book and for your expertise and professionalism in the editing process.

To the many intercessors, especially my Monday morning Bible study group of ladies in the winter and my Tuesday prayer group in the summer: thank you for every prayer prayed that extinguished the darts of the enemy I endured while writing this book.

Most of all, thank You, Lord Jesus and Father God, for trusting me with Your message to all. And precious Holy Spirit, thank You for every thought, every word that has been penned in this book, for the glory of God.

CHAPTER I

THE BATTLE IS REAL

To be sober, be vigilant, your adversary,
the devil walks around like a roaring lion
seeking whom he may devour.
1 Peter 5:8 (NKJV)

"Pastor Tim..." my husband Jon mumbled through tears of pain as he walked in the door, "was let go!" One Sunday morning, without an explanation, a clue, or any kind of notice, the elders at our church dropped this unexpected bomb on our congregation. For the past thirteen years, Pastor Tim had been the shepherd of the church we attended and loved. How could this be? Many speculated, but the mystery remained.

And just like that, Pastor Tim (name changed due to privacy) went from being Moses, ready to lead us into the promised land with a huge expansion before him, to Joshua, ready for the most unexpected battle of his life.

But as Joshua faced this unforeseen future, the Lord gave him both a hope and a promise when He said, "I will never leave you nor forsake you" (Josh. 1:5b).

Being a part of Pastor Tim's journey, along with many who stayed by his side in prayer and intercession, we watched God fulfill the same promise to him. When his world fell apart, our pastor and friend humbled himself and cried out to God, and God proved faithful.

In the biblical story of Moses and Joshua, which begins near the end of Deuteronomy (Chapter 31), Joshua, inherited a battle he never imagined—a battle he didn't feel equipped to fight on his own. He had followed God under Moses's leadership, and after the great leader's death, the Israelites looked to Joshua as their new leader. Moses left big shoes to fill.

Even though the Lord told Joshua, "I will give you every place you set your foot, as I promised Moses" (Josh. 1:3), God didn't promise an easy journey. It may sound exciting to receive such a word from the Lord, but Joshua surely remembered an earlier trip he had made with eleven other spies into Canaan. Afterward, they reported that they had spied "giants in the land" (Num. 13:32).

Have you been there? Has God ever spoken a promise or given you a glimpse of what He desired for your life and, on the surface, it sounded thrilling? Were you ever commissioned for a position like Joshua's, and you couldn't wait to begin? Though the position might seem appealing, just like Joshua, you could be about to enter enemy territory on the way to your "promised land."

Battles You Can See
Growing up in the sixties and seventies, we had family-oriented TV shows like *Leave It To Beaver*, *Bonanza*, and (who could forget) *Father Knows Best*. But along with those lighthearted sitcoms, like Joshua, we faced a battle—the Vietnam War.

After watching our favorite programs, the evening news kept us updated with the latest reports of the day: stories about horrific bombings, plane crashes, and the daily count of the soldiers who died while fighting for our country. During "Vietnam," the most significant causes of death in the US armed forces were small arms fire (31.8%), booby traps including mines and frags (27.4%), and aircraft crashes (14.7%).[1]

When reading the above article about the Vietnam War, what caught my eye was the significant amount of lives that were lost due to landmines and hand grenades. When you consider that the amount of US fatal casualties was close to 58,000 this means that 15,892 of our men died from land mines and hand grenades.

The North Vietnamese were notorious for planting land mines. Our soldiers carefully made their way through the fields of Vietnam, praying they would not step on a bomb hidden below. Graphic photos and video footage shown so many years ago of those who lost their limbs and even their lives still haunt me today.

Hidden Battles

Although that part of our history ended in 1975, we face a different type of war in our society today. We live with the war on terrorism. We hear or view horror stories of suicide bombers who attach bombs to their cars and drive with a deadly mission into schools, synagogues, and even crowds of people.

The Boston Marathon bombing on April 13, 2013, was an attack our country will never forget. Multiple bombs exploded near the finish line as many of the runners finished their race. Three people lost their lives, including an eight-year-old boy, and 260 people were injured.[2]

Invisible Battles

The other war we face is an invisible war. We face battles every day in the spiritual realm. Satan is at constant war with God, and we are in the middle. We are the ones who must walk so carefully and run so purposefully, all the while hoping nothing will explode in our face.

The apostle Peter warns us to "be alert and of sober mind. Your enemy the devil prowls around like a roaring lion looking for someone to devour. Resist him, standing firm in the faith, because you know that the family of believers throughout the world is undergoing the same kind of sufferings" (1 Pet. 5:8-9).

So, knowing that, how do we avert Satan's bombs? How do we avoid the attacks of the enemy?

Fight Your Battles

For our first defense, we must believe the war is real. We must not see ourselves living in a fairy-tale world. Even though they walk the Christian walk and talk the Christian talk, some people refuse to believe Satan is real.

He is.

He is as real as the ground we stand on. But what we stand on will make all the difference. Are we standing on the Word of God, or are we on sinking sand?

Knowing the Word of God and what it says about warfare is our defense. Knowing our authority—the authority Jesus Himself passed down to us—is of utmost importance. Satan is the master deceiver, and the last thing he wants to see is us walking in our God-given destiny.

Please don't get me wrong: I am not giving Satan any credit here. But take a look in the book of Job, especially at the first chapter, which tells the story of Satan coming to God to have a conversation with Him.

> One day the angels came to present themselves before the LORD, and Satan also came with them. The LORD said to Satan, "Where have you come from?"
>
> Satan answered the Lord, "From roaming throughout the earth, going back and forth on it."
>
> Then the LORD said to Satan, "Have you considered my servant Job? There is no one on earth like

him; he is blameless and upright, a man who fears God and shuns evil."

"Does Job fear God for nothing?" Satan replied. "Have you not put a hedge around him and his household and everything he has? You have blessed the work of his hands so that his flocks and herds are spread throughout the land. But now stretch out your hand and strike everything he has, and he will surely curse you to your face."

The Lord said to Satan, "Very well, then, everything he has is in your power, but on the man, himself do not lay a finger." (Job 1:6-12a)

Face Your Battles

What does this mean for you? Does it mean you stop doing what God has called you to do? Does it mean you watch others make strides and accomplishments while you step back in fear?

No! That's the coward's way out. We must go forward, believe what the Word of God says, and not allow the enemy to take away the promises God has for us.

Look at Joshua again. He knew there were giants in the land but did it stop him? No. He went for it. I love the first chapter of Joshua, which reads:

After the death of Moses, the servant of the Lord, the Lord said to Joshua son of Nun, Moses' aide: "Moses my servant is dead. Now then, you and all these people, get ready to cross the Jordan River into the land I am about to give to them—to the Israelites. I will give you every place where you set your foot, as I promised Moses. Your territory will extend from the desert to Lebanon, and from the great river, the Euphrates—all the Hittite country—to the Mediterranean Sea in the west. No one will be able to stand against you all the days of your life. As I was with Moses, so I will be with you; I will never leave you nor forsake you. Be strong and courageous, because you will lead these people to inherit the land I swore to their ancestors to give them." (Joshua 1:1-6)

Although they had earlier seen "giants in the land," Joshua and one other of the spies, Caleb, wanted to go for forward and take possession of what God promised. Like the other spies, they saw the bad—the giants. But they also saw a land flowing with milk and honey, and they knew from the past the power of the Lord God whom they served. With God on their side, they believed they would be able to conquer the giants and dwell in the land the Lord had promised. As it turned out, of the twelve spies, only Joshua and Caleb lived to set foot in the land God had promised them.

We, like Caleb, Joshua, and our Pastor Tim, face battles every day. We can be assured that just as God was with them, He will also be with us. He will not leave us to fight alone. He assured Joshua that He would neither leave him nor forsake him. We can stand on the same promise today.

Win Your Battles
Looking back on Pastor Tim's journey, I see that God has been ever so faithful. Although Pastor Tim never imagined beginning a new church, God directed, and he followed. Week by week, the church grows. As God led Joshua to his promised land, He guides Pastor Tim to lead our new congregation.

During a meeting with Tim, I was amazed as he shared the Scripture that enabled him to go through his roughest times: "As I was with Moses, so I will be with you; I will never leave you nor forsake you." God is real and faithful to do what He says He will do!

My prayer for you is that as you read on, you will know not only that the battle is real, but that *in the name of Jesus* you have the power to win your battles.

Each chapter will give you the tools needed to fight, along with a few personal experiences I have encountered. I also pray you will be encouraged as you hear real-life stories where I, along with fellow intercessors, prayed through dire circumstances, and God showed up time after time.

Get your seat belt on—get ready—let's go!

Reflection

Take a few minutes and reflect on what you just read.

- Do you believe Satan is real?
- As Joshua faced his giants, what are the giants you are facing today?
- Do you believe God can be with you as He was with Joshua?
- Are you ready to discover how?

Meditate or journal for the Lord to equip you on your journey to your promised land.

Memory Verse:

To be sober, be vigilant; because your adversary the devil walks around like a roaring lion seeking whom he may devour.

1 Peter 5:8 (NKJV)

THE BATTLE

The battle is very real
it's time for you to see.
The battle is very real
against the enemy.

He comes to kill and to steal
his goal is to destroy.
He disregards your calling
and robs you of your joy.

He's a liar and a deceiver
he sets you up to fall.
He's crafty in his doings
he's master of them all.

So, let's discover the power
God has given to you.
That you'll be able to conquer
all Satan tries to do!

CHAPTER II

TICK - TOCK BOMBS GOING OFF

For God has not given us a spirit of fear, but of
power and love and a sound mind.
2 Timothy 1:7

Just as the landmines in Vietnam were buried to destroy our soldiers, the enemy has one goal in mind. We are his target, and he devises strategic plans to destroy us.

Fredrick Downs Jr. became a living example of the devastation a "Bouncing Betty" causes after one exploded beside him. His platoon was only taking a short march across the sand dunes to set up their ambush for the day. Lieutenant Downs followed behind two of his men as they carefully moved forward to check the trail in front of them for booby traps and mines.

As they turned and waved to Downs with an "all clear," his foot slipped backward a fraction of an inch, hitting a mine's trigger mechanism. He never heard the explosion as black powder and dirt engulfed him. His body flew through the air. He threw his arms out in front of him as a reflex motion to balance himself and, in doing so, he saw the horror of a jagged white bone sticking out of the stump where his left elbow had been.

Six other men also suffered horrific effects, and the dunes looked like a blood bath.

After serving five months in Vietnam, this twenty-three-year-old soldier rode a roller-coaster of surgery and pain. Later, Lieutenant Downs received numerous awards for his service, including four Purple Hearts and induction into the Officer Candidate School Hall of Fame at Fort Benning Infantry School.[3]

Our battle may not be as physical or as horrific as Lieutenant Downs's, but in the spiritual realm, Satan works in this exact same way, using subtle tactics to deceive us.

To understand what this spiritual battle is all about, we must first know our enemy. Our enemy is Satan. He will do all in his power to destroy our body, soul, and spirit. If he can accomplish this, we will be of no use in the kingdom, nor will we be able to fulfill our God-given destiny.

Satan's tactics are subtle. He knows what it will take to push our buttons. He'll attack our health, family, and our marriage. He even attacks us at work where we spend most of our time. Whatever way he can, he will try to keep us off the path God has so carefully laid out for us.

Spiritual warfare is real—I know. Through a story from my own life, you will see how the enemy works and how spiritual warfare can change our lives and our mission.

Due to a change in my life, I began to battle with high blood pressure—something I had never experienced before. Previously, whenever I visited a doctor, they would examine me and question my low blood pressure. I never worried because this was normal for me.

Then everything changed. With a pain in my side, my husband rushed me to the hospital, where the doctor ordered numerous tests. My blood pressure spiked higher than usual. On the day they discharged me, it kept registering higher than the doctors wanted to see it, so to be comfortable, he put me on blood pressure medication.

My whole life spun out of control. Fear crept in. I gave the enemy all he needed to kick the door open and feed my fear, which he used to steal my peace, my joy, and even my walk with the Lord. I was up night after night, afraid that if I dared to lay my head on the pillow and fall asleep, I'd never wake up again. I became a basket case, to put it mildly.

I Knew God Loved Me, But...

I knew God loved me. I knew all the promises in the Bible. Still, I stepped into the minefield of fear, and without even realizing it, I allowed it to control my mind, body, and emotions. I now refer to this time as "the year from hell."

What I didn't understand was that fear is a spirit, a spirit I allowed to take control. When my blood pressure began to rise, instead of calling on God immediately, I would imagine it rising higher and higher.

After three trips to the ER and one specific night where my blood pressure peaked at 210/110, I knew this merry-go-round had to stop. I stood in the kitchen at about 3:00 a.m. and spoke directly to the spirit of fear. I began to take the authority I knew God had given me.

Earlier that week at church, the guest speaker spoke a word over me. She said I had allowed fear to come in and to destroy my life. When I heard it, I denied it. How could that be, I thought. I know the Word of God. I know the promises and all He has for me.

But as we learned in chapter one, we must first admit there is a battle and know who our enemy is. Just as the soldiers in Vietnam had to know their enemy and what they needed to fight their battle, so must we.

Time to Turn the Tables

After my third trip to the ER, I decided that I wanted my life back. I'd had enough. After all those sleepless nights, I declared that this state of passivity was over! I recognized the battle and faced the enemy. I understood it as a real thing. I saw fear as a tool Satan had used successfully against me *because I acted on it.*

So, I spoke directly to that spirit of fear. I called it by name; I commanded it to leave in the name of Jesus and never to return. Then, I continued to speak the Word of God over myself.

My dear believer, I want you to understand the power you have in the Word of God. That night, I claimed promise after promise over myself. "I can do all through Christ who strengthens me," I said (Phil. 3:19 NKJV). "God has not given me a spirit of fear, but of power and love and a sound mind"[4] (2 Tim. 1:7 NKJV). On and on I declared, including the words from Paul's letter to the Corinthian church, which says, "We demolish arguments and every pretension that sets itself up against the knowledge of God, and we take captive every thought to make it obedient to Christ"[5] (2 Cor. 10:5).

The more I focused on God's promises and not on the numbers of my blood pressure reading, the more I felt God's peace.

Was it easy? Not really. But I stuck with it until it became a new norm. So it will be for you, too, as you learn to reshape your thinking unto the Word of God.

The Key
The key to the battle is learning how to recognize the bomb before it explodes. That bomb may be different for each person, but for me, it meant addressing the fear before it had a chance to run wild. I had to learn to speak to my mind and to take it to the Lord before I started to imagine the worst.

After that night, before I went to all the usual places my mind would take me, I started going to the source. I went straight to fear and addressed it. "You will not have authority over me tonight!" I declared. "You will not take away my sleep! You will not control me! If God is for me, who can be against me?" I spoke to fear with the authority given to me in the name of Jesus and saw myself freed from that ugly thing until one day I was finally free. Fear no longer had its vicious hold on me!

Does it come back to haunt me now and then? Indeed, it does. But I have decreed and declared that fear will never destroy my life as it did before. I know we have the power; it is the same power that raised Jesus from the grave. As we read in Romans 8:11: "And if the Spirit of him who raised Jesus from the dead is living in you, he who raised Christ from the dead will also give life to your mortal bodies because of his Spirit who lives in you."

Stand in Power

When we know Jesus and understand what He did for us on the cross, we will believe that the power Jesus used to rise from the grave is the same power we have inside of us.

As I talk about that power, let me reiterate one thing: the word *know*. It's one thing to say it, but it's another to know it deep down inside of you.

When we are born again, the Holy Spirit comes to live inside of us. The same Spirit with the same power that Jesus had. My friend, if you take away anything from this book, I pray you will understand the power that lives inside of you. Paul wrote in his letter to the Ephesians: "Now to him who is able to do immeasurably more than all we ask or imagine, according to his power that is at work within us."[6]

The same power I called upon during my battles is available to you. However, you must first recognize its presence before you release its power to the fullest capacity.

The power given to us through the Holy Spirit will destroy any bomb the enemy has planted. Isn't that interesting? The enemy has minefields to trip us up, but God has given us a greater power. He has given us His Holy Spirit to live within us so that no matter what the enemy sends our way, our power is greater. You must know it, and then you must use it to detonate the enemy's bombs.

From the Mouth of Babes

My grandchildren love to dress up as superheroes. When I walk into their house, I never know who will greet me at the door. It could be Superman, or maybe Captain America, or perhaps the latest one, Thor.

They love watching movies with their superheroes; they can't get enough. Sometimes when I walk into their family room, I'll ask, "Cesare, are you watching that same Thor movie again?" When I can recognize a move from just one scene, you know it's a repeat.

One day I realized that the core of their make-believe movies is the same as our world today: good vs. evil. Even my three-year-old grandson will answer me when I comment that I might not like one of the characters. "No, Grandma," he'll say. "He's a good guy. You can't say you don't like him."

Even as young as three years of age, our children know good from evil. Hollywood displays it right there on the big screen and in our living rooms. Kids learn to fight at such a young age. As I watch their movies, I see the weapons of war at work—clashes, clings, and dings from swords, knives, and any other weapon they find.

The End. You Win.

It's the same as in the Bible: the good guy wins in the end! Sometimes we are so deep in our battles, we forget the words at the end of the book.

> Then I saw a new heaven and a new earth, for the first heaven and the first earth had passed away, and there was no longer any sea. I saw the Holy City, the new Jerusalem, coming down out of heaven from God, prepared as a bride beautifully ·dressed for her husband. And I heard a loud voice from the throne saying, "Look! God's dwelling

place is now among the people, and he will dwell with them. They will be his people, and God himself will be with them and be their God. 'He will wipe every tear from their eyes. There will be no more death' or mourning or crying or pain, for the old order of things has passed away." (Revelation 21:1-4)

God has an ultimate plan. While on the island of Patmos, the apostle John penned it beautifully in what we now call his Book of Revelation. Unfortunately, when we are faced with a trial, it's challenging to smell even a scent of victory.

That's the time to defeat the lies of the enemy with the promises of God. To cry out to God and ask Him for the strength to hold on. Time to grab the Word of God—the "sword of the spirit" as Paul calls it—and claim the Scriptures. They are the inspired words of God and they are our weapons of destruction. Just like my grandkids and their superheroes, we not only have the costumes to put on, but all the gear that completes the wardrobe. They have matching helmets, a shield for Captain America, and a box-like hand for Iron Man to quench the darts or anything that sails his way.

We have the same ammunition to win our battle. But because our war is invisible, we don't need swords or guns to fight. Our warfare, as Paul tells us in Ephesians, is not carnal. Rather, we have weapons for the pulling down of strongholds.

For though we live in the world, we do not wage war as the world does. The weapons we fight with are not the weapons of the world. On the contrary, they have divine power to demolish strongholds. We demolish arguments and every pretension that sets itself up against the knowledge of

God, and we take captive every thought to make it obedient to Christ. (2 Corinthians 10:3-5)

Well, there it is, the sweet taste of victory. Follow me along to the next chapter, where we will continue to discover the power that lives within!

Reflection
Take a few minutes and reflect on what you just read.

- Do you know your enemy?
- Can you specify what he uses to set you off?
- Think back to a specific situation in your life and ask yourself, who or what did he use to upset me? How did God turn things around?
- What is your favorite Scripture to combat the enemy?

Meditate upon it and ask God to empower you in whatever you're facing today.

Memory Verse
For God has not given us a spirit of fear, but of power and love and a sound mind.
2 Timothy 1:7 (NKJV)

TICK TOCK WHAT'S GOING OFF

Tick tock bombs waiting to go off
from the rise of your day.
Walk my child so carefully
trust Me to clear the way.

For as the soldiers in the day
had one to go before.
I will cause the spirit in you
to search Me more and more.

Then as you search Me, you will learn
the power of My Word.
And you will answer what need be
by all that you have heard.

You will answer one-two-three
or four or five or six.
You will quote My Scripture then
to avert each bomb that ticks.

CHAPTER III

THE POWER OF PRAYER IN THE FIELD

What no, eye has seen, what no ear has heard, and
what no human mind has conceived the things God
has prepared for those who love him.
1 Corinthians 2:9

Life enables us to experience all sorts of emotions. The joy of first love. The heartache of losing a loved one. The thrill of a rollercoaster ride.

Even the seasons, set in place by God, share their wonder with us through our senses. With the first dusting of snow, children—even adults—dash outside to dance beneath its feathery chill. The smell of spring flowers reminds us that, after death, there is life...and it is sweet. And what about the warmth of a summer breeze against an ocean's tide? Or the magic of autumn's leaves falling in colors so brilliant we can scarcely name them?

But what if there's more?

We walk in the natural realm. We see with the natural eye and hear with the natural ear. We feel the snow's chill, we smell the flowers, we see the ocean waves crash and autumn's leaves fall. We hear them crunch beneath our feet as we walk on the carpet they've made.

But what if there's more?

What if God has more for you? What if there are places God wants to take you where you can experience Him like never before?

"Eye has not seen. Ear has not heard" is the beginning of the Scripture above, but as you continue on, it says that "no mind has conceived what God has prepared for those who love Him."

Do you want more of what He has for you? This can be frightening, but remember, God loves you. He holds you in the palm of His hand. He wants to be the one to deliver you from whatever you are going through. He has given you ways to experience His love through prayer and petition, but also through warfare. As you've probably already discovered, we walk every day among the minefields Satan has planted *intentionally* for us. But take heart. God knows where they are, and He wants to enable us to walk through and stay clear of those traps.

How does He protect us? For one, it is by calling others to pray even if we cannot pray for ourselves. This is a humbling experience, especially when we know that the Spirit of God has alerted someone to pray for us and they have answered the call.

This is but one example of God's love *for us*.

There are many kinds of love. There is the love of a parent, the love of a spouse, or the love of a friend. But when we experience the love of God, His perfect love, it leaves us speechless.

Obedience is the Key
One morning, the Holy Spirit woke me at about three o'clock. I knew I had been woken to pray. Although I didn't know who the prayer was for, the Spirit revealed I was to pray for someone with pain in their legs. I remember feeling as if they were falling into a deep, dark hole.

My prayers got louder and more intense. I woke up my husband and said, "Please pray with me. I don't know who it is for, but someone *somewhere* is in trouble. They are in desperate need of prayer."

I prayed intently in the flesh, then back and forth in the Spirit. Although I did not know who the prayer was for, I could feel that they were in a deep battle, and I felt like it was a battle for their life.

About an hour later, I felt a breakthrough. I was not able to go back to sleep, but the extreme burden had left. Whomever I had prayed for had been released from the hold upon their life.

The next morning, I attended a board meeting for a local ministry. After greeting one another, my friend Marty began to share with us something she had experienced during the previous night. Her words left me speechless. I sat in silence; chills trickled up and down my back.

She was the one! She was the one I had warred for. The more she shared, the more I believed the recipient of my prayer had been her. When she started to describe that she felt like she was being pulled into this dark hole, I was sure—it *was* her!

When she finished, I shared what I had experienced. She asked me what time it had happened, and sure enough, her trial was at the exact time I had been warring in the Spirit, decreeing and declaring this precious child of God to be free from the torment they faced.

Let Go, Let God

I have learned that it's not necessary to know whom we are praying for. It's also *not* essential to know the full extent of what we are to pray for. As we step out in obedience, the Spirit leads and guides. Sometimes I've been led to pray for hours without knowing for whom, but in obedience, I prayed until I felt a release from the Spirit.

When the Spirit prompts you, pray. Sometimes when you are obedient to pray and you cry out in the Spirit, He will reveal things you need to know such as people, places, and mysteries. Sometimes, He'll even bring a specific person to mind and prompts you to pray for them, just pray and allow Him to lead.

Remember, the Spirit searches the things of God, and then He shows them to you.

> *These are the things God has revealed to us by his* **Spirit.** *The* **Spirit searches all** *things, even the deep things of God.*
> 1 Corinthians 2:10 (NIV, emphasis mine)

Someone I respect once told me that "all means all, and that's all it means." The Holy Spirit of God searches the heart of God. He searches *all things*, even the deep things of God, and then He reveals them to you.

Through experience, I've discovered that when we try to figure out what is going on, when we try to analyze what we're feeling, we hinder the Spirit. It's like our flesh comes in and intervenes with the Spirit of God, and the two begin to tangle. So now, when I'm prompted to pray, I continue to do the battle for "whomever" and leave the rest to God.

Why do I share this with you? Because I believe if we are going to pray effectively and productively, we need to know and understand the depth of God's love. First for us, and then for others. When we are willing, He will use us to pass His love to others. Marty needed help. God could have supernaturally set her free. But, because I ask Him every day, "Lord use me," He used that opportunity to draw both Marty and me closer to Him.

Do You Want to Be Used by God?
Do you believe He can use you? If so, ask Him. The biblical story of the young lad Samuel exemplifies this perfectly. One night, Samuel heard someone calling his name. He thought it was the priest Eli, with whom he lived at the temple. After Samuel's third time going to Eli and saying, "Here I am," Eli realized the voice had come from God. Sometimes we are much like Samuel; God

called him *three* times before he understood that the voice had come from God.

Has He been calling you? Does He have a specific call on your life? Do you say, "Maybe He can use others, but I don't see how He can use me?"

Think again. If God can use a young boy such as Samuel, or a woman such as me, then He can use *you*.

Above all else, God requires our availability. I don't usually get up in the middle of the night. But when God calls, I know it, because He awakens me in such a way that I'm wide awake and ready for battle. When that kind of stirring happens, I know it's time to get up. Soldiers may be in a dead sleep, comfy in their barracks, but when the call comes to rise and head out for emergency battle, they can't roll over, pull the covers over their heads, and let others do the job. *They* have been called to this task. We, too, have a part to play. Battles rage day and night for family and friends and strangers around us and we must be ready. If we love the Lord and our hearts are set for Him to use us, we must get up and go into battle *whenever* the call arises. We must be obedient to heed to the Spirit of God. During this time, it's important to listen to where He is leading and then to follow. He might urge you to pray for a particular situation. He may even direct you to *go* somewhere. You may not know why initially. There could be someone you need to speak to or a message you need to receive. One thing is for sure: unless you are obedient, you will never know.

Holy Spirit, Speak

Can we commune directly and speak with the Holy Spirit? Yes, we can. When I began my Christian walk, a friend gave me a Bible. She told me I needed to call upon the Holy Spirit before I started reading. At the time, I looked at her like she had two heads, but after so many years, oh how I get it: *He's real.*

The Holy Spirit is the third person in the Trinity, and He is waiting to commune with us daily. He is a significant part of our spiritual life and He does not want to be silent.

One afternoon I was in a department store when the Spirit of God came over me, telling me someone there needed prayer. I wasn't sure who, so I silently asked, "What's up? Who needs prayer? Where do you want me to go?"

I wasn't looking for jewelry, but that was where I heard Him say to go. So although I was contemplating buying a wallet, I strolled over to the jewelry counter and asked the clerk there if she could ring up my purchase.

Oh, she smiled with the brightest smile. "No problem," she said. As we began to chat, she shared with me it was only her second day back to work after two years of dealing with cancer.

How was one to know? She was radiant and smiled brightly. But she was scared to death on the inside, she told me. Only the Spirit of God could have known that. He knew she needed someone at that very second to lift her up and to encourage her that everything would be all right.

She also shared that she was worried because her husband was at home, concerned for her. He had not wanted her to go back to work, fearing she'd have a relapse. But she knew she needed to return, if only for herself. She needed to get back into the workforce and trust God that He would take care of her and her family.

So, there I was, right in the center of all the precious stones Kohls has to offer, embracing one of God's beloved children. We called on our heavenly Father to wrap His loving arms around His daughter, to assure her He was right there with her. Oh, it was a glorious moment. Not many compare.

As I returned to my car, I bowed my head and smiled. "Oh, Holy Spirit," I began. "You knew she needed help. I didn't go in to buy this wallet; I could have found one anywhere. But You knew how desperate that young gal was as she cried out for help. She just needed someone to affirm to her everything was going to be okay."

Not Ability, But Availability

Hearing from God is all a part of listening and being available. I could share story after story of when the Lord directed me to to a specific store, to stand in a particular line in the grocery store, or to sit in one particular seat on a plane so I could lead a seatmate who lived in fear and desperation to the Lord.

You never know what's behind a smile, but God does. And that's why He needs you and me. That's why we need to be available and to say, as Samuel said, "Speak, for your servant is listening" (1 Sam. 3:10b). Samuel grew to adulthood and became a great prophet of Israel. Like him, you never know the places God will take you once you're willing to go!

Earlier, I asked, "What if there is more?"

After hearing these stories, I hope you know there is. Although you are in an earthly body, when you heed yourself of the Holy Spirit, He will take you to that other realm. He will guide your spirit by His Spirit as to what to do and where to go so you may help another.

Now turn the page and discover the weapons God has provided for you as you go forth in battle—for you, and for others as well.

Reflection

Take a few minutes and reflect on what you just read.

- Is God calling you?
- Can you remember a specific time where He called you? What did you do?
- Do you believe there is more? If so, are you prepared to dig deeper and see what God has for you?

Take a few minutes today to see what God might be saying to you.

Memory Verse

> *What no, eye has seen, no ear has heard, and what*
> *no mind has conceived the things God has prepared*
> *for those who love him.*
> (1 Corinthians 2:9)

DO YOU BELIEVE

*No eye has seen, no ear has heard
what God intends to do.
But when you stop, look and listen
He'll gently speak to you.*

*Oh, He'll reveal the hidden things
when you begin to pray.
He'll reveal what you need to know
For one who's in dismay.*

*Yes, He has many things to say
and places for you to go.
Where He now wants to use you
and His Spirit's free to flow.*

*So to you, I ask the question
do you believe there's more?
That God's prepared for each of us
and we have so longed for?*

CHAPTER IV

KNOW YOUR WEAPONS

*The weapons we fight with are not the weapons of
the world. On the contrary, they have divine power
to demolish strongholds.*
2 Corinthians 10:4

Have you ever heard of the Goldilocks Principle? The Goldilocks Principle is a concept taken from the classic children's tale, *The Three Bears*. The idea, or principle, states that "just the right amount," and can be applied to various things. Astrology, biology, child development, medicine... the list goes on and on. Can you believe one of our Bible stories, David and Goliath, falls under the Goldilocks Principle?

As the tale goes, a little girl named Goldilocks stumbled into a cute little cottage in the woods. She was famished. To her surprise, she found three bowls of porridge on the wooden table. But the first bowl's contents were too hot. The second, too cold. But the third bowl of porridge was "just right," and she ate it all up. After she finished eating, she felt a little tired, so she went into the living room, where she found three chairs. The first one, she declared, was "too big." The second was also "too big." But the third one was "just right." Unfortunately, when she sat on it, the chair broke. Still tired, Goldilocks decided to go upstairs for a nap. She crawled up into the first bed, ready to fall asleep, only to say, "This bed is too hard!" So, she decided to try the second bed, but quickly she mumbled, "Oh, no, this bed is too soft." Then she spotted a third bed. As soon as she laid down, she cuddled up, pulled the covers over her, and whispered, "This one is just right."

In the story of David and Goliath (1 Samuel 17), Saul and the Israelites went to fight the Philistines. The Israelites occupied one hill and the Philistines another, with the Valley of Elah between them. Saul seemed confident they'd triumph until the nine-foot giant, Goliath, came out of the Philistine camp to challenge the Israelite army. Saul and his men gasped! They were dismayed and terrified at the sight of their enemy. Surely, they declared, "This battle is too hard."

Goliath, clothed in his heavy-duty armor, saw himself as a champion, and believed there was no one powerful enough to kill him. For forty days he continued to taunt the Israelites, saying, "This day I defy the armies of Israel! Give me a man and let us fight each other" (1 Sam. 17:10). And, for forty days, the Israelites trembled beneath the weight of the threat.

Until a young shepherd named David showed up with food for his brothers who were a part of Saul's army. While talking with them, the great giant came down and declared his threats once more. David, of course, heard him. But even more so, he watched his fellow Israelites flee in fear.

David asked a simple question: "Who is this uncircumcised Philistine that he should defy the armies of the living God?" (v. 26). When Saul heard that David had made such a declaration, he called for the young man to be brought to him.

"Don't worry," David told Saul. "I'll take on the giant."

Of course, Saul, seeing the size, the youth, and the inexperience of David, said, "You'll be killed."

But David had experience Saul knew nothing of. During his time working as a shepherd, he'd had to kill a bear and a lion to protect his father's flock. In David's mind, anyone who defied God was subject to be treated like the predators he'd already taken on. After sharing this with Saul, the king replied, "Go, and the LORD be with you" (v. 37).

When David went out into the valley of Elah, he was dressed simply and carried only his staff, five smooth stones from the nearby stream which he placed in a pouch, and his sling.

When Goliath first saw David and realized that he was only a boy—and one not dressed for battle—he balked. "Come here," he said, "and I'll give your flesh to the birds and the wild animals!" (v. 44).

But David knew that while Goliath might have been "too big," and he "too little," the LORD was "just right." He shouted back at the giant, "All those gathered here will know that it is not by sword or spear that the LORD saves; for the battle is the LORD's, and he will give all of you into our hands" (v. 47).

As Goliath charged David, the young shepherd-turned-soldier placed one smooth stone into the sling and, with a single blow, killed the great giant. But it wasn't the stone that carried the power, and David knew it. The others feared Goliath, but David did not because he carried his secret weapon, which was *knowing* the power of coming to battle in the name of the LORD, his God.

Survival Is the Key

One evening while visiting my grandkids, Cesare amazed me with his latest invention. He and his friends love to play in the woods. Although my daughter warns him about animals who might be roaming around, it's all about the adventure for him.

Cesare called me to the door before he came in for the night. I wondered why he hesitated and waited outside, until he held up a crusty old stick and shared his treasure. "Look, Grandma, look what I made."

He'd created a spear from a stick about as tall as himself with a triangle-shaped object attached to the end.

"How did you get the metal piece to stick?" I asked him.

"Easy, Grandma," he responded. "I took the gum I was chewing, and I used it."

Although it was funny to me, he looked at me with all seriousness and responded, "Just in case a fox came to attack us, I could use my spear and kill him."

I knew that if a fox dared to attack my ten-year-old grandson, the little makeshift spear would not have saved his life. However, even at such a young age, survival was inherently important to Cesare. God placed it in him and God has placed it inside you and me. It's part of our DNA.

No matter our battle—be it cancer or some other form of sickness, be it an ongoing battle resulting from a divorce, a wayward child or other relationship issues, or working a job filled with contention—everywhere we turn, it's a struggle to survive.

Dress the Part

Remember our soldiers in Vietnam? Can you visualize how they dressed to fight the enemy? Army fatigues, heavy combat boots, their faces often painted black—whatever it took to remain invisible. They walked through the jungle with M-40s strapped across their chests and a handful of grenades tucked inside their belts.

Now, a soldier wearing his dress greens might look a little different. He'd have on a crisp, green button-down cotton shirt, with perfectly pleated dress slacks, a shiny patent-leather belt, and spit-polished black shoes—not to forget his firm-brimmed cap to complete the look. If you saw the two soldiers side by side, you'd know who was on their way to an award ceremony and who was ready for battle.

Weapons are a significant part of the battle. Now that we know what a soldier would wear, what should you and I look like when we engage in a spiritual battle? The Old Testament tells us that when soldiers went into battle, those who led in praise went first (2 Chronicles 20:21).

Do you begin with praise when you face a battle? Although it may not always make sense, God wants you to begin our battles with *praise*. We can try to fight on our own and with our own handmade weapons, but God desires to be acknowledged first. This is our first area of defense. Like in the story of David and Goliath, God wants us to praise Him. He wants us to acknowledge that it will not be us, *but Him,* who will fight *and win* the battle.

Your Greatest Weapon

Years ago, while going through a tough situation, I wasted so much time trying to figure everything out. I'd replay conversations over and over in my mind even before they'd happen. *If she says this, I'll say that. And if she says that, then I'll respond with this.* On and on I'd rehearse, trying to manipulate the outcome.

Have you ever been there? You wanted to put yourself in the other person's head, trying to figure out precisely what they were thinking and how they would respond. If you're like me, it never worked out the way you planned. You probably didn't say half of what you thought you'd say, and neither did the other person. What a peace-stealer!

During my quiet time one day, the Holy Spirit opened my eyes to a Scripture that changed my life forever. "The horse is made ready for the day of battle, but the victory rests with the LORD" (Prov. 21:31). I printed the words on flowered paper and placed it on my desk to remind me to *step back.* From that point on, I decided I was not going to allow Satan to steal the peace God had for me.

Once I discovered what the Word said, my thinking changed. The Holy Spirit showed me I could not fight the battle on my own. I needed Him, His wisdom and discernment, to fight, and then stand strong. God wanted me to hold my ground. But, also, my heart needed to be right. My focus needed to be centered on God's will, not mine. Once I understood the battle was His, He opened my eyes to the second half of the Scripture, which is the key to victory: "But the deliverance is of the LORD."

We can do nothing without God. We cannot achieve victory on our own. No matter what battle we face, His wisdom, guidance, and power are essential.

Because God is infinite and omniscient, He knows the outcome of every situation before we do. He has the blueprint for our life, our family members, and our loved ones. No matter how bad we want to see something happen, our job is to pray, leave it at the cross, and then follow God's instructions.

Gear Up

The Scripture for this chapter tells us our weapons are not of the world.

So, what are those weapons? Indeed, they are not like the M-40s our soldiers carried, or a grenade tucked away on the hip. Our greatest weapon is the Word of God, which brings with it divine, supernatural power. Since our weapons are supernatural, we can be dressed in our Sunday best or an old pair of jeans and go into battle. Many of the battles I fight happen while I am at home. I always tell my husband I should alert our neighbors if they hear screaming; we are not fighting...it's me going into battle.

Our power comes from knowing what the Word of God says. When we speak the Word and declare the Word, the atmosphere begins to change around us. Now we're ready for battle.

Strongholds keep us in bondage. As we pray, the Holy Spirit reveals the strongholds to us. When we speak the Word of God over them, they come falling down. Once the strongholds are torn down, then it is time to go in clean out what is there.

When we go into battle for someone else, begin by thanking the Lord for what He can do. For what *He has the power* to do. Then we must ask the Holy Spirit for His help. Ask Him to reveal what bondages hold our prayer-focus. As we do this, the Holy

Spirit speaks to our heart to show us what needs to be removed, and in the removing, how to set someone free.

Let the Battles Begin

Once we've removed the strongholds, it's time to replace the negative thoughts with positive ones. Begin by decreeing positive words over your friends. Remember, "'Not by might nor by power, but by my Spirit,' says the LORD Almighty" (Zech. 4:6). His power enables us to do our part and leave the outcome to God.

Speak your prayer-focus's name and proclaim that they are free in the name of Jesus. Use Scripture. If you know the chapter and verse, say it.

I know NAME HERE is free because it says in the book of John, "So if the Son sets you free, you will be free indeed" (John 8:36).

There is nothing like allowing the Scripture to do the work. A well-known preacher once said, "There is life in the Word." Knowing this and believing it makes all the difference in the world. Never forget: *The deliverance is of the Lord.* Quoting His Word back to Him reminds God to keep His promises, but it also gives us rest.

Ephesians 6 tells us that the Word of God is the Sword of the Spirit. "Take the helmet of salvation and the sword of the Spirit, which is the word of God" (Eph. 6:17). That, my friend, is our sword to go into the enemy's territory, slay the giant standing in our way, and go forth in victory! His Word is sharper than any two-edged sword; it cuts between the flesh and the morrow (Hebrews 4:12). It's there for us. All we have to do is pick it up and use it.

A little side note about the sword Paul referred to in Ephesians: it was not a huge sword. On the contrary, it was a short-bladed dagger. Soldiers in his time stuck it directly into an enemy and went for the kill.

We have the the same power. The Word of God goes into the enemy for the kill. It dispels the darkness and brings the light. So, next time you are ready to pray for someone, remember you will *not* win by the ways of the world. You will win your battle with the Word of God as the spiritual forces of evil are torn down and victory is released from the heavenly realm.

We saw the same within the story of David and Goliath. David declared, "All those gathered here will know that it is not by sword or spear that the Lord saves; for the battle is the Lord's, and he will give all of you into our hands" (1 Sam. 17:47). David knew this to be truth. He spoke it. And it was so.

Reflection

Take a few minutes and reflect on what you just read.

- Do you know what your secret weapon is? David had five stones and the Word. What has God given you?
- Do you ever feel inadequate to fight for a loved one?
- What is the most potent battle you've faced? Reflect on how the Lord brought you through. Then, praise Him.

Meditate or journal and ask the Lord what weapons you have to fight your battles.

Memory Verse

The weapons we fight with are not the weapons of the world. On the contrary, they have divine power to demolish strongholds.
(2 Corinthians 10:4)

THY WORD

Weapons come in all shapes and sizes
yet what is right for you?
What do you need to accomplish?
What do you want to do?

What will destroy the enemy
from lurking at your door?
What will you use to avert him
and give him ground no more?

Oh could it be a Beebee gun
Or maybe a stone or two?
Something to shew him forever
and keep him clear from you.

The power you need is in the Word
that's your authority.
To speak what God has given you
to defeat the enemy!

CHAPTER V

THE GENERAL OF INTERCESSION—THE HOLY SPIRIT

Surely you need guidance to wage war,
and victory is won through many advisers.
Proverbs 24:6

"Del, I believe I have a word for you," said the voice on the phone. "The Lord says, 'Dust the sand off your feet and move on.' I don't know if it means anything, but the Lord impressed upon me to call and share this word with you."

For the past year I attended a secular critique group for writers. The members wrote manuscripts with mainstream content, but mine contained spiritual content. I wanted to stick it out and remain a light, but whenever I read my work, the ungodly spirits reared their ugly heads. Instead of critiquing the structure or providing helpful feedback, they attacked the content.

One evening my husband noticed my negative attitude. "What's up?" he said. "You leave here, and you're in a great mood. Then you return home and there's a spirit I don't recognize coming out of you."

I knew he was right, but I refused to admit it. Yet, the phone call from a dear friend led me to believe God knew how the enemy used those in the writer's group to discourage me and distort my spiritual walk. God used her to tell me, "You're done. Move on."

Although this was early in my spiritual walk, it left a lasting impression: I witnessed the vital importance of the Holy Spirit. I loved attending this critique group, but the enemy used it to distract me from God's purpose for my writing. I had silently battled the ungodly spirits attacking me week after week, but just in time, the Holy Spirit impressed upon a dear friend to call me and lift me out of my battle.

We need the power of the Holy Spirit in every battle we face. either by Him speaking to us directly or, as in my case, through a friend. He is the third person of the Trinity, and He longs for your fellowship. He desires greatly to lead and guide you into battle. He is your general in intercession.

First Things First

As we enter into battle (prayer), it's essential to see that our heart is right. When we enter the battle in the flesh, we might try and manipulate the outcome rather than allowing God to have His way.

That is why it's so important to commune with the Holy Spirit before we enter in. He does not come to condemn, but He will gently convict us of our intentions. When He sees that our heart is right, then we are ready for battle. There will be no envy, no jealousy; only a pure heart calling out and standing in the gap for another.

David gave us an example in Psalm 51. "Create in me a clean heart, O God. Renew a loyal spirit within me. Do not banish me from your presence, and don't take your Holy Spirit from me. Restore to me the joy of your salvation and make me willing to obey you" (Ps. 51:10-12 NLT).

A clean heart is a result of confessing anger or bitterness against a brother or sister, or confessing our sins against God. If we allow the sin in our heart to ooze and fester, the enemy will use it to keep a wedge between God and us.

The Bible tells us that the "fruit of the Spirit" is love, joy, peace, longsuffering, kindness, goodness, faithfulness, gentleness, and self-control (Galatians 5:22-23a). Those are the qualities we must possess when praying for another.

A few years ago, the Lord called me to pray for someone, a child, who was hearing voices. Through prayer and fasting, I sought the Lord to know what my part was in freeing this young girl from such oppression. About that time, a friend gave me a book for Christmas entitled *Breaking the Power* by Liberty S. Savard. Who but the Lord would have known that her gift would be my aid in this upcoming battle?

I went to a pastor and friend and shared the situation. He prayed for me and helped guide my steps. In love, he explained step-by-step what I could do to free this child of the spiritual tormenter.

I knew some things about spiritual warfare, so I knew I wanted the same assurances the disciple Peter asked for in Matthew 14:22-29

> Immediately Jesus made the disciples get into the boat and go on ahead of him to the other side, while he dismissed the crowd. After he had dismissed them, he went up on a mountainside by himself to pray. Later that night, he was there alone, and the boat was already a considerable distance from land, buffeted by the waves because the wind was against it.
>
> Shortly before dawn Jesus went out to them, walking on the lake. When the disciples saw him walking on the lake, they were terrified. "It's a ghost," they said, and cried out in fear.

> But Jesus immediately said to them: "Take courage! It is I. Don't be afraid."
>
> "Lord, if it's you," Peter replied, "tell me to come to you on the water."
>
> "Come," He said.[7]

What happened next holds the key for me. When the wind started blowing, Peter took his eyes off Jesus and focused on the storm. He became afraid and started to sink. He cried out "Lord, save me!" (v. 29).

Immediately, Matthew records in verse 31, Jesus reached out his hand and caught him.

I wanted to walk with the same assurance as Peter, knowing that even if I started to fear, Jesus would reach out His hand and catch me, too.

After my meeting with the pastor, I followed his lead. I fasted and prepared my body to hear what the Lord would say. I knew the necessity of putting aside my wants and desires so I could listen to the Holy Spirit.

Crucial Preparation

The day arrived when I was to go pray for this little girl. It was encouraging to me that her parents were open to whatever the Spirit led us to do. My only plan at this point was to listen to the Holy Spirit and to go forward in what He said.

The night before, I visited them, I was awakened by the Holy Spirit. He directed me to read a specific chapter in the book *Breaking the Power* that deals specifically with the soul.

> Your soul—your mind, will, and emotions—is meant to be in perfect alignment with God's will and purpose...(Savard 50). [8]

Our un-surrendered soul wants no part of surrendering to God. The Holy Spirit revealed that it was the soul-ties of this little girl that needed to be broken...broken *never* to return.

I read it, highlighted as He directed, then read it again until I fell asleep. I prepared my body, mind, and soul to help this child. I wanted to be qualified for what God had called me to do. My pastor emphasized that spirits are real, and I must be strong in how I dealt with them.

Daylight came, and I was ready. "Set the stage, Lord," I asked. "Not too early and not too late," I added. "In Your time, just lead me in whatever I need to do." Besides the help of the Holy Spirit, I called upon three powerful prayer partners to stand in the gap and pray as I went about that day. I did not go in unprotected. I knew that if I asked, they, along with my pastor friend, would be in prayer for me.

When the time was right, we started. At first, I felt resistance. Then, as I continued in prayer, the spirit in her began to taunt me. I knew I had touched a nerve when I prayed *in* the Spirit. I do not remember the exact words or Scriptures I quoted, but I do know that the Holy Spirit gave me a boldness like I'd never had before.

As I spoke directly to the spirit, he did not like it. He started to answer me back. I recalled the words of the pastor...*I could not be afraid.* I had to speak with boldness and I did just that. Out of my mouth came one Scripture after another.

Before I knew it, she fell back on the bed. It seemed she lay there for an eternity, but I heard the Spirit say, "Just leave her. You pray and allow me to minister to her." That I did. I just stood over her and silently continued to pray in the Spirit.

Deep down, I feared that the evil spirit would jump out and harm me. But the pastor had said, "Del, you are the one in control. When you come in the room *in the name of Jesus*, you have all authority, and you cannot show them you are afraid."

He was right.

When the little girl came to, she was radically changed. Even her dad noticed it. Her countenance changed, and her face radiated. The tormenter would never torture this child again!

As directed, I thoroughly anointed the entire house with a new bottle of pure virgin olive oil. I anointed every single door and window in the entire house. The family joined in as we went from room to room, praying in the name of Jesus and covering the entire house with the blood of Jesus while listening for the voice of the Holy Spirit.

We stopped anywhere the Holy Spirit said to stop and pray more intensely. He even spoke of things that needed to be removed permanently from their home. Without asking, they removed every piece I pointed out.

To this day, I still remain in contact with her family and praise God that there has never been another incident of the child hearing voices. The Lord truly set this child free, and the tormenter has never come back.

When I was a child, my family loved to play a game called Taps. My five siblings and I would sit in a room and my mom would grab a small pan and spoon from the kitchen. One of us would walk out of the room, and the other five would find something to move or rearrange.

When the person came back into the room, they would have to figure out what we moved. The fun was in the name of the game. Mom would tap the pan with each step they took. The closer they came to the moved item, the faster and the louder she'd tap. If they veered off in the wrong direction, she'd stop and wait for them to turn around.

Learning to listen for the voice of the Holy Spirit is much like in that game. The key is listening. In quietness, we hear His still, small voice. He prompts us to do things just as He did when we anointed the home to see where spiritual doors could have been opened.

He leads us to places He needs us to go, but if we aren't listening, we could miss the very thing God sent us to do.

Wait for the Gift

> On one occasion, while He was eating with them, he gave them this command: "Do not leave Jerusalem but wait for the gift My Father promised, which you have heard Me speak about. For John baptized with water, but in a few days, you will be baptized with the Holy Spirit." (Acts 1:4-5)

Jesus told His disciples to *wait* for *a gift*. Have you ever thought of the Holy Spirit as a gift? In the book of Acts, you can see why God calls it a gift. Only through the power of God could I fight the spiritual battle to free this child from tormenting spirits.

A gift is something precious, something given in love. It is not forced upon us. But once we receive the Holy Spirit, it will become one of the most powerful tools or weapons we possess.

You can see from my experience how the power to heal came through the promptings of what the Holy Spirit directed me to do. But the difficult part is found in the waiting (v. 4).

Imagine what the disciples experienced. We are on the other side of Pentecost and Jesus's command. We know how the story goes and how it ends. But do you think they understood what they were waiting for—even though Jesus had explained it?

> But the Advocate, the Holy Spirit, whom the Father will send in My name, will teach you all things and will remind you of everything I have said to you. Peace I leave with you; my peace I give you. I do not give to you as the world gives. Do not let your hearts be troubled and do not be afraid. (John 14:26-27)

Yes, they had many conversations with Jesus. He had told them that the Holy Spirit would teach them all things, remind them of everything He said, and give them power. But how could they fully comprehend something they had never experienced?

They could only rely on the words Jesus had spoken to them. We must do the same. We must not run ahead, but rather wait to hear what the Spirit has to say to us. If we do, He will lead us into all truth, just as Jesus promised. He will guide us before, during, and even after our battles. But the key is to wait. If I hadn't waited for the opportune time to pray for that child, if I had just gone on my own, who knows where she'd be today. I had to sit. I had to read. I had to meditate on the Word of God, then stop and listen. I had to *hear* what the Holy Spirit said so that I could be guided by Him.

There's power in waiting. An extraordinary power comes upon us when the Holy Spirit comes to live and activate his power within us. But there's even a greater power in waiting.

Lying in Wait

I had the opportunity to go hunting years ago. Not something I ever imagined myself doing, but yes, I sat for hours in the cold waiting for an innocent young deer to cross our path. I must say it was quite the experience, but once was more than enough.

Looking back, it was all in the waiting. Not a sound. Not a creak. I could only hear myself breathing. But then, suddenly, we heard the crackling of leaves that indicated that the deer was off in the distance.

Although we didn't kill her, we had the perfect opportunity as she crossed our path. That's how it is in battle. Quietly, we seek the Spirit. He leads us to quiet our minds and hear His voice. Then, just like hearing the rustling of leaves underfoot, we know when it's time to take action.

Now that you know your general of intercession, follow with me as we travel to the next chapter and learn how to armor up for the fight.

Reflection

Take a few minutes and reflect on what you just read.

- Do you believe the Holy Spirit can speak to you?
- Do you understand the power you have once you activate His power within you?
- Are you ready to sit and wait for Him to lead and guide your life?

Meditate or journal as the Holy Spirit speaks to you.

Memory Verse

But the Advocate, the Holy Spirit, whom the Father will send in My name, will teach you all things and will remind you of everything I have said to you.
(John 14:26)

BREATHE ON ME

Precious Holy Spirit of God
there is no other like You.
To lead and guide throughout my day
in everything I do.

I know before My Savior left
He promised You would be.
An Advocate to all who asked
so now please come to me.

I ask that You would enter in
that I'd not be alone.
That You would speak from deep within
the words I need to know.

And You would show me everyday
the path God has for me.
That I could be all He desires
and set the captives free.

CHAPTER VI

KNOW YOUR AUTHORITY

Finally, be strong in the Lord and in his mighty power. Put on the full armor of God, so that you can take your stand against the devil's schemes. For our struggle is not against flesh and blood, but against the rulers, against the authorities, against the powers of this dark world and against the spiritual forces of evil in the heavenly realms.
Ephesians 6:10-12

"What am I going to wear today?" With the change of seasons and temperatures starting to drop, it was time to change my wardrobe from shorts and tees to jeans and sweaters.

As I glanced around my closet, I heard the Spirit speak to my heart, "And what about your spirit-man? What will he wear today?"

God gently reminded me that just as you need to get ready for the cooler temperatures of fall, it's important to learn how to cover your spirit-man also.

It might not be with a quilted jacket, bulky gloves, and a scarf around your neck, but you do need a covering. In Ephesians 6, the apostle Paul describes to us piece by piece the armor of God we are to wear to battle the enemy. He relates each piece to how a Roman soldier dressed for battle.

The Belt of Truth

The first piece of essential armor for fighting spiritual battles is the belt of truth. "Stand firm then, with the belt of truth buckled around your waist" (Eph. 6:14).

The belt of truth strengthens our core and enables us to stand firm. We cannot stand firm in anything if we do not know what we are standing for. Do you know your core beliefs? Do you take a stand for the truth of God?

It is essential to understand the truth of what the Bible says. As we read the Scriptures daily, they reveal the truth of who we are in Christ. Once we know who we are and *whose* we are, we can stand in confidence.

When the enemy attacks (and he will), it is imperative that we call upon the Holy Spirit. He enables us to reach beyond our current situation and helps us recall the promises of God. We can say, "I am a child of God! I am freed by the precious blood of the Lamb! I am a child of the King!"

The Holy Spirit helps us think on every Scripture that states the truth of who we are in Christ.

A few years ago, as I struggled with my health, my belt of truth unraveled, and fear gripped my heart. I found a plaque in a gift store that read: "Finally, brothers and sisters, whatever is true, whatever is noble, whatever is right, whatever is pure, whatever is lovely, whatever is admirable—if anything is excellent or praiseworthy—think about such things."

These words helped strengthen my core and guided me back on the road to freedom.

Satan, often called "the deceiver," wanted me to focus on the negative. He wanted me to believe I'd never get better. I had to reprogram my mind and force myself to think positive thoughts. Every morning I'd read this verse and ask the Lord to help me throughout the day. Whenever I'd start to dwell on the circumstance, I'd turn my thoughts to Him.

The Breastplate

The next piece of armor Paul describes is the breastplate. "Stand firm, then, with the belt of truth buckled around your waist, with the breastplate of righteousness in place." (Eph. 6:14). The breastplate protects the heart. Oh, how the enemy would love to damage that very precious part of us with hurt, abuse, depression, and other emotions designed to bring us down.

No one can survive with a damaged heart. Years ago, my younger brother, while in the middle of a stress test, had red flags go up. The doctor stopped the test and immediately sent him to the hospital. After a heart cath followed by an emergency bypass surgery, the doctor explained to him that his arteries were ninety-five percent blocked; he was lucky to be alive.

The heart is unable to function correctly if there is an obstruction of the flow of blood to it. We are the same spiritually. When there is a blockage in relationships with family or other loved ones, we are unable to function as God intends. Hurt damages the heart. We often say we have a "broken heart" after a painful breakup, a misunderstanding, or harsh words, especially from those we trust *not* to hurt us.

Hurt is a tool the enemy uses as an open door to create havoc in your life. If our heart is damaged, how can we help one another? This leaves us with a handicap, and we will not be able to help others. That is why the breastplate is so crucial: it protects our most vital organ. "Above all else, guard your heart, for everything you do flows from it," Solomon admonished in Proverbs 4:23.

At the end of Paul's description of the breastplate, he calls it "the breastplate of righteousness." Yes, the breastplate is for protection, but it also enables us to walk in righteousness, not prideful or boastful of who we are in ourselves, but rather who we are in Christ.

In Ephesians 4, Paul explains that we are to put off our old selves and put on the righteousness of Christ. "You were taught, with regard to your former way of life, to put off your old self, which is being corrupted by its deceitful desires; to be made new in the attitude of your minds; and to put on the new self, created to be like God in true righteousness and holiness" (Eph. 4:22-24). The belt of truth must be secure around our waist to guard us in who we are. During the time of Paul, the breastplate weighed the soldiers down. The Roman soldiers needed the belt to hold it up.

Doesn't it all make sense? Think about it; the breastplate resembles our righteousness in Christ. What a heavy weight to bear! But the belt of truth holds up that heavy piece of armor, and when it is securely buckled around our waist, we can walk confidently in who we are in Him.

The enemy would love to cower us down with lies about ourselves and with feelings of low self-esteem and total inadequacy. But once we know who we are in Christ and we believe that the risen Christ dwells within, we have the power to push past the lies of the enemy and move on.

The Gospel of Peace

To avert spiritual landmines, we need to shod our feet and walk in peace. This is where the enemy would especially love to trip us. When everything is breaking loose or breaking apart, it's difficult to walk in peace.

I am the first to say that time and time again, I've failed in this area. When things go wrong, I find it easy to lose my cool and allow anger to flare up. Some people have passive anger; some active. Someone with passive anger keeps it inside. Most times, they shut others out, leaving them to deal with the situation on their own. But the rejection stirs up a wave of even greater anger.

On the other hand, it's easy to know when someone with active anger is mad! Everyone knows when something is not going that person's way! I believe this is why Paul tells us that we are to stand "With your feet fitted with the readiness that comes from the gospel of peace" (Eph. 6:15).

If we cannot learn to walk in peace, we will fall into the trap of the enemy every time. Our emotions, rather than the Holy Spirit, will lead us. When something goes wrong, our reaction will be a sad illustration of the gospel we have planted in our heart. Instead of living and walking out in peace, we explode and make way for the enemy.

Remember Paul's list in the "Fruit of the Spirit"? "But the fruit of the Spirit is love, joy, peace, forbearance, kindness, goodness, faithfulness, gentleness, and self-control. Against such things there is no law." (Gal. 5:22-23). Learning to walk in the Spirit and produce that fruit takes time. We don't learn to do it overnight—none of us. I know it's difficult to not be hard on yourself when you fail, but understanding that this is a daily growing and maturing in your Christin walk enables you to go from glory to glory.

Shield of Faith

Now, let's be honest. Have you ever bit your tongue, kept the peace, and experienced the sweet smell of victory only to have a flaming arrow fly in from another direction? This is how the enemy fights. He is vicious in his battles. He is the adversary who comes to kill, steal, and destroy (John 10:10).

Thank God, then, for the next piece of armor—the shield of faith. "In addition to all this, take up the shield of faith with which you can extinguish all the flaming arrows of the evil one" (Eph. 6:16).

Oh, how the enemy doesn't want us to know about this piece of the armor *or* how to use it. Many of the superheroes my grandchildren watch on TV or on their handheld devices carry a shield—especially Captain America. You will rarely see him without his powerful shield, held to protect his life. Sometimes he holds it by his side. When the enemy sails a weapon his way, he responds in an instant. He takes his stand, digs his feet into the ground, reaches his arms out in front of him, and holds his shield clear to his chest. He refuses to let anyone attack him and win.

God gave us the same power, but we must remember to carry our shield and carry it always. Being sensitive to the tricks of the enemy is essential. We must be quick to see when he's sending one of his flaming arrows of pain, or fear, or guilt, or anything he thinks he can use to take us down. Just like Captain America, we must hold up our shield of faith to stop the flaming darts from reaching their destination.

The shield, like other pieces of armor, has a twofold purpose: one is protection and the other is to help us *stand* in faith. In my early Christian walk, I'd hear messages on faith. "Faith is an action word," preachers said. I didn't get it, because I considered faith a *thing*. Something you either had or you didn't. Now, twenty-plus years later, I've *lived out* faith. And I know that it's not just enough to read the Bible; you must believe it too. Look at the eleventh chapter of Hebrews.

Hebrews 11 is called the "faith chapter." I love how it begins: "Now faith is confidence in what we hope for and assurance of what we do not see—" (Heb. 11:1). Sounds a bit ironic, doesn't it? How can you be sure of what you don't see? But as we continue to read the entire chapter, we can't help *but* believe, especially after reading the stories of our spiritual forefathers and mothers who walked in blind faith.

We read about Abel, who offered God his best sacrifice; Enoch, known as one who pleased God, who was taken from this life without tasting death; Noah, who out of obedience built an ark and saved his entire family.

Let's not forget "Father Abraham." First, he had the faith to believe he would have a son in his much-later years. And, when he finally did, Abraham was willing to offer him as a sacrifice out of obedience, unaware God had a spotless ram on the other side.

Each one of them had blind faith. Your shield of faith is all about what you can't see. You cannot see faith. Faith is exercised when you believe in the promises of God. When the enemy sends his fiery darts to bring doubt and destruction into your life, your faith fizzles them out!

Helmet of Salvation

I'm not one to live my life around sports, but now and then I'll sit beside my husband and watch a game or two, usually the play-offs. Football and baseball are my favorites.

Can you imagine a football game where players entered the field without a helmet? The way they get hit, banged around, and knocked to the ground, there wouldn't be any players left by the time the Super Bowl rolled around. The helmet is their protection; it covers their eyes, ears, nose, mouth, and everything in between. Without their helmets, players would not survive the game—or life—for long.

Paul says we can have the same protection. "Take the helmet of salvation and the sword of the Spirit, which is the word of God" (Eph. 6:17).

Satan's favorite plan of attack is against your mind. He loves to make you feel unworthy, useless, and incapable of doing all God created you to do. If you allow him, he'll hold you captive by your thoughts. If he can control your mind and keep you from knowing and understanding the Word of God, he has won the battle. He would love to do nothing more than have you believe you are the victim and not the victor.

Remember, my friend, there is victory in Jesus. In the book of John, Jesus says, "I am the way and the truth and the life. No man comes to the Father except through Me." (John 14:6). The enemy whispers lies as a way of controlling our thought process. His motive is to keep us from believing the truth and calling the name of Jesus. We remain the victim and not the victor when we believe false accusations.

The mind controls the emotions. If the enemy can control your mind, he will control your emotions. Once he starts to attack, he is relentless. He is not happy to steal only our peace; he wants all—our body, soul, mind, and spirit. Just like it is for a football player, the helmet is essential to shield us from injury.

The second half of the Scripture found in Ephesians says that the helmet is the "helmet of salvation," which is our identity in Christ. Our salvation is obtained through the life, death, and resurrection of Jesus. The helmet is a continual reminder of our freedom in what He has done for us.

Satan will try to steer us off the path God has laid so carefully and so beautifully. Paul shares in Galatians: "It is for freedom that Christ has set us free. Stand firm, then, and do not let yourselves be burdened again by a yoke of slavery" (Gal. 5:1). Jesus declared victory for us. We must, in turn, trust Him with the process.

The Sword of the Spirit

Now for some action! Every other piece of armor is *defensive*. The sword is *offensive,* in other words, used for the kill. Every soldier who goes into battle needs an offensive weapon.

Paul wrote: "...and the sword of the Spirit, which is the Word of God." Today we refer to the Bible as the Word of God, which means that those words within it are our sword. When I took this to heart, I said, "If it is a sword, then I have the power to use it and to do damage!"

We have power when we speak and decree the Word. We defeat the arrows and cast down the lies of the enemy.

The kind of sword the Roman soldiers used was not a large sword that they swung about. No, it was a small, knife-like sword, able to dig in and destroy. This is good because, sometimes, it's the small things that cause more damage. In this case, the Word of God may seem like a small thing (just a word), but it's the small dagger used to kill. We must believe that the Word of God has that power. *Power*—incredible, working power as we speak it and believe every word we proclaim!

> For the word of God is alive and active. Sharper
> than any double-edged sword, it penetrates even
> to dividing soul and spirit, joints and marrow; it
> judges the thoughts and attitudes of the heart.
> (Hebrews 4:12)

God's Word is truth, and in it there is great power.

Now we have all the pieces of the armor. And, just as we dress ourselves before heading out the door, we must remember to dress the spirit-man. To keep him covered. As we do, we should speak aloud to the enemy and take our authority back.

As you head onto the next chapter, you'll understand the power we have in our words. You will learn how to speak and how your words will lead you to victory every time.

Let's go!

Reflection

Take a few minutes and reflect on what you just read.

- Can you name each piece of armor?
- Do you understand how each piece will protect you?
- Do you believe the armor will make a difference next time you face a problem?

Meditate or journal and ask the Lord to fill you with the confidence you need for whatever you are going through. Where do you need this protection today?

Memory Verse

Finally, be strong in the Lord and in his mighty
power. Put on the full armor of God, so that you can
take your stand against the devil's schemes.
Ephesians 6:10-11

DRESS THE PART

It's knowing your authority
that will take you through.
It's knowing your authority
for what you need to do.

It's putting on each piece you need
from your head to your feet.
To keep you covered well in battle
as you fight the enemy.

Yes, from the helmet to the breast
and the belt round your waist.
Along with the sword of the Spirit
as you bear the shield of faith.

And don't forget to shod your feet
with the gospel of peace.
That you can walk as Jesus walked
And succumb the enemy.

CHAPTER VII

WORDS ARE WEAPONS

*Ask, and it will be given to you; seek and you will
find; knock, and the door will be opened to you. For
everyone who asks receives; the one who seeks finds;
and to the one who knocks, the door will be opened.*
Matthew 7:7-8

"If I take one more step, I think I'm goanna die," I said to a friend after our walk one evening.

"Well, before you do," she sarcastically remarked, "let me know what kind of flowers you want."

I didn't understand what she was saying at first, but then I remembered how many times she had reminded me that I would eat the fruit from my words.

Back then, I didn't understand how I needed to weigh my words. Come to think of it, I never heard teachings on the power of my words and how they'd project what would be. Although I laughed at her dry sense of humor, I knew what she meant. I got it. Sometimes we say foolish things, and we don't mean the words at all.

Words can either make or break a situation. That's why it's essential to be careful about what we say. Every time we open our mouths, it says something about who we are.

When children speak, we can see a glimpse into their family life. Just hang around a playground and you will see the type of upbringing they have and the amount of respect they have toward their parents and other adults.

As adults, we're the same. If we listen in on someone's conversation, we can discover so much about them. We can discern what they believe and how closely they walk with the Lord. Just sit on a plane next to a total stranger and you'll see what I mean. Sometimes, before the wheels lift off the ground, you'll have a pretty good idea of the kind of person you'll be sharing the flight with, especially if they are on the phone. For the child on the playground or the person on the plane, what we see in the flesh is their physical appearance, but once they open their mouths to speak, we will instantly know who they are in spirit. "The words of the mouth are deep waters, but the fountain of wisdom is a rushing stream" (Prov. 18:4).

Breaking Strongholds

In the previous chapter, we discussed our weapons: "The weapons we fight with are not the weapons of the world. On the contrary, they have divine power to demolish strongholds" (2 Cor. 10:4).

Strongholds are the areas of captivity where the enemy is holding us or a loved one captive. Sometimes we are aware of it, and other times we are not. The first thing to do is to seek the Holy Spirit and see where there are regions of captivity. Usually, when we're praying for one another and we ask the Holy Spirit, He will reveal what is holding someone in bondage.

Sometimes it goes back to childhood. It's important to have this kind of information so that we know what to pray about; we cannot deliver someone just because we feel we think we know what's holding them back. The Holy Spirit must reveal this, showing how to pray so that He can set the person free. "These are the things God has revealed to us by His Spirit. The Spirit searches all things, even the deep things of God" (1 Cor. 2:10).

A friend of mine, Chris, began having terrible nightmares, after which she would awake with pain throughout her body. One night, she said, it was as if someone continued to poke her all over with pins and needles. Not sure what to do, she called a close friend and me to pray. The Holy Spirit revealed witchcraft.

A short time later, the person whom we suspected started bragging to my friend, Chris, how she used a voodoo doll to torture her ex-husband. Instantly Chris remembered the experience she had during the night; she wondered if this person was the one who was possibly using witchcraft against her. Chris and I prayed and decreed and declared that whoever was doing this had no power. We prayed in the name of Jesus and pleaded the blood of Jesus over Chris and her entire household. Although Chris never discussed the ordeal with her friend, she never had another incident again. Witchcraft is real. When the Holy Spirit gives revelation, it's important to remember that we have the power to proclaim the Word of God and, in speaking, to break its spell.

How do we break free? Or, how do we help others? The Word of God is our number one weapon. We fight the enemy by quoting Scripture directly to Satan and telling him where his place is—under the feet of Jesus. Then, we plead the blood. Satan hates when he hears us mention the precious blood of Jesus.

After His baptism by John, Jesus spent forty days in the desert. After this time, Satan tried to tempt Him. He promised Jesus that if He would bow down and worship him, he, Satan, would give Jesus all the kingdoms of the world.

> Again, the devil took him to a very high mountain and showed him all the kingdoms of the world and their splendor. "All this I will give you," he said, "if you will bow down and worship me." (Matthew 4:8-9)

Jesus answered him with the Word of God. He said, "Away from me, Satan! For it is written: 'Worship the Lord your God and serve him only'" (Matt. 4:10). Jesus quoted directly from the book of Deuteronomy with both power and authority. The same thing Satan wanted from Jesus is what he wants from us. His goal is to sway us from worshiping God to worshiping him.

If Jesus, who is God, needed to quote the Word back to Satan, how much more do we need to know the Word of God to speak it back to the enemy? If we do not *know* what the Word of God says, we will fall into believing other voices around us.

The end of this story in Scripture leaves us with hope and encouragement for whatever we face: "Then the devil left Him, and angels came and attended Him" (Matt. 4:11).

Some translations say the angels *ministered* to Him. Whatever we face, either for ourselves or a loved one, what a comfort to know God will send His ministering angels to come and care for us in our time of need.

Words Are Weapons

The key to breakthrough is to become more aware of what we say. What comes out of our mouths will make all the difference in our lives and the lives of others around us. Words can either loose or bind. Solomon tells us in Proverbs 18:21 that life and death are in the power of the tongue.

Think about that. Our tongue has the power to *agree with* life and something that will bring us life, or to *agree with* death and something that will result in destruction.

I heard a teaching years ago where the pastor said you couldn't get clean and dirty water out of the same cistern. Either the water is clean, or it is unclean; it can't be both. That makes so much sense, and it should be taken into consideration when praying. We can't say something positive about who God is and what we believe He can do, then walk out of our prayer time and doubt what we've said. Speaking the truth with authority and making declarations of what will be is what will bring about transformation. Our words cannot be snared by disbelief.

Scripture says, "For the word of God is alive and active. Sharper than any double-edged sword it penetrates even to dividing soul and spirit, joints and marrow" (Heb. 4:12). Understanding the Word's power will remind us to pick up the sword and use it in the heat of the battle.

It's all about speaking positively. It's important to see ourselves as the victor and not the victim. When we know God is for us, we are more apt to approach any given situation as the winner.

Jesus gives us *all* the authority we need. "I have given you authority to trample on snakes and scorpions and to overcome all the power of the enemy" (Luke 10:19).

In the book of Luke, Jesus sent out His disciples with orders to go only where they were welcome. When they returned, they told Jesus that even the demons submitted to them in His name. Jesus explained to them, then, that He "saw Satan fall like lightning from heaven" (Luke 10:18). He was telling them, as He is telling us, that Satan does *not* have authority over us. He *is* a defeated foe. Authority is something delegated, and Jesus has delegated the authority *to us* to speak to the enemy and defeat the powers of darkness in His name.

Prayer Is a Weapon

In our last chapter, we covered the armor of God. The final piece of armor is prayer. It is not a piece Paul tells us to "put on," as with the other pieces, but something *to do*. He tells us to always pray in the spirit: "And pray in the Spirit on all occasions with all kinds of prayers and requests" (Eph. 6:18).

So, if prayer is part of our armor to extinguish the darts of the enemy, it must become the first thing we turn to in times of trouble. Many times, people say, "Well, I guess I can pray." No!

Our victory comes by acknowledging prayer as the *first* resort, not the *last*.

Prayer is our time to commune with God. It's not where we provide a laundry list telling God what we want Him to do; it's a time of fellowshipping with Him. When you have a specific person you are praying for, you bring that person and their need to God.

It pleases God when we pray His promises back to Him and believe in faith that He is the one to answer the need. Psalm 91 is a perfect example.

> Surely he will save [Name] from the fowler's snare and from the deadly pestilence. He will cover [Name] with his feathers, and under his wings [Name] will find refuge. (Psalm 91:3-4)

Insert the person's name that you are praying for into the Scripture. Make it personal. Like sending a greeting card...you address it to your friend or your loved one. Do the same when you pray Scripture over them. Make it personal and call the promises out to and for them. If they need protection, proclaim: "For he will command his angels to guard [Name] in all [his/her] ways" (v. 11). Find the Scripture in the Bible that speaks to what they are going through. With 365 promises to choose from, at least one will apply.

In addition, we are told not to pray in vain or amiss, hoping to hit the bullseye, but to be firm in our stance and in our words and not to waver.

> But when you ask, you must believe and not doubt, because the one who doubts is like a wave of the sea, blown and tossed by the wind. That person should not expect to receive anything from

the Lord. Such a person is double-minded and un-stable in all they do. (James 1:6-8)

The War Is On

Recently, my niece, Laura, was expecting her first baby. During her labor, my sister-in-law Sue kept me posted. My prayer partners and I remained in prayer as she continued to text us and let us know what was going on.

She started her labor late in the evening. Finally, at 11:30 the next morning, baby Jesse arrived. We celebrated and praised God for the miracle of another addition to our family. The next afternoon everything changed when I received a text from my sister-in-law that read: "Pray. Baby's in trouble." Although I didn't know what was wrong, I prayed. I didn't alert anyone else until I knew more.

At ten o'clock in the evening, my sister-in-law called and said the doctors thought the baby had pneumonia or meningitis. After we talked, I did the first thing which came to mind. I flipped opened my laptop and started to search for information on infants with these illnesses. Fear gripped my heart with each word...until...

Until I heard the Holy Spirit speak to my heart, saying, "Close the computer and go to WAR!"

I knew it was serious. I went to my desktop computer, and I did something I had never thought of doing before—I put a request on my Facebook page for anyone who could pray to contact me. In faith, I believed that even if it was 11:30 at night, someone would respond.

Immediately my phone dinged. A dear friend responded to join me in prayer, and from that time on until the wee hours of the morning, calls and texts continued. Fellow warriors warred for this precious little baby. We had to go forth in faith. Together we continued to pray and decree *life* and *not death* for the child.

We stood firm in faith and decreed prophetic words over him as the Holy Spirit led.

The next morning as I joined fellow writers for our monthly critique group, another text flashed across my phone: "No pneumonia! No meningitis!!!!"

Tears of joy (along with fresh mascara) trickled down my face. God had heard our prayers and moved heaven and earth to begin to heal that little child from the inside out.

Is This Your Battle to Fight?

Sometimes God lets us know when a specific battle is too big for us to fight alone. Even though someone asks us to pray, we might think we're ready to do battle without another soldier. Whatever the need, just as with my niece, as soon as my sister-in-law called and I heard there was a problem, I was ready to go.

Before we let our emotions run wild, we must stop and ask God if this is something to pray about on our own or with the help of others. Ask Him to guide and let you know your part.

Years ago, our city was preparing for its first Spiritual Warfare Conference. I was very young in the Lord, so I was unaware of what spiritual warfare was all about. One evening after a meeting with the planning board, I prayed for the leadership team on my way home.

I didn't know that you do not speak directly to Satan and tell him your plans without having a covering; I let him have it. About one o'clock in the morning, I awoke in fear with a heavy, dark presence in my room. I could not move.

I called my spiritual mom, Jan. I cried for her to come over and get me. Before she arrived, I finally got out of bed and turned on every light in my apartment. Once we got settled back in her condo, she explained that this battle *is* real and how I should have gone about dealing with it. Her words of wisdom created a secure foundation for who I am today.

The most important thing she shared with me was that we must pray and plead the blood of Jesus whenever we engage in such a battle. This is what we did; over and over, we continued to plead the blood of Jesus until peace finally filled her place.

The blood has power. When Jesus shed His blood at the cross, Satan was, from then on, a defeated foe. In the Old Testament, the Lord directed the Isralietes to sacrifice bulls, goats, and sheep to atone for their sins. But we are on the other side of the cross. We have victory in Jesus. Jesus died and shed His blood for our sins, and Satan takes no delight when we remind him of that and proclaim the truth. That evening was a real eye-opener to what spiritual warfare is all about.

Now that we know the power of our words, let us go on and learn how Satan desires control of our minds.

Reflection
Take a few minutes and reflect on what you just read.

- Do you understand the power of your words?
- After reading this chapter, do you have a better understanding of what spiritual warfare is? Can you see the importance of being covered when you pray?
- What has God shown you regarding your prayer life? How will it help you?

Meditate or journal for the Lord to guide you in your prayer life.

Memory Verse
Ask, and it will be given to you; seek and you will find; knock, and the door will be opened to you. For everyone who asks receives; the one who seeks finds.
Matthew 7:7-8

I SAID WHAT?

Words are a powerful weapon
so important that we see.
That every word we choose to say
will surely come to be.

The tongue has an ability
to bring life or death to you.
So weigh your words so carefully
In all you say and do.

For once a word is spoken
it can't come back you know.
So always try to speak in love
And let God's goodness flow.

CHAPTER VIII

THE MIND FIELD

*For our struggle is not against flesh and blood, but
against the rulers, against the authorities, against
the powers of this dark world and against the spiritual forces of evil in the heavenly realms.*
Ephesians 6:12

Afootball field is a vast grassy terrain. When the players file through the tunnel and the crowd rises to their
feet, the game begins. Both sides are geared up and
ready to go.

Our mind is the same—a vast terrain where Satan loves to
play. When we open ourselves up to negative thinking, he sends
his players in to do what he does best: deceive.

When we are down, when we are out, the field of our mind is
green for the enemy to come in and do significant damage. In the
book of Romans, Paul states: "For all have sinned and fall short
of the glory of God" (Rom. 3:23). And in 1 John we are reminded
that "if we confess our sins, he is faithful and just and will forgive
us our sins and purify us from all unrighteousness" (1 John 1:9).

Satan only wants us to remember the first Scripture—*we have
sinned.* He does not want us to know the second one. He wants
us to believe no one has messed up as bad as we have. No one has
done what we have done. Then, as he mocked Jesus in the desert,
he does the same to us. He taunts and asks, "Who do you think

you are? Do you really think God will forgive you?" Satan tries to demean us and make us feel we are less than.

If he can mess with our minds and get us to think less of ourselves, he wins. His goal is to destroy our integrity, which is the opposite of God's goal. While Satan wants us to see ourselves from the bottom, never able to achieve all God has, God wants us to see ourselves as victors. He wants us to see ourselves as He created us, with a plan and a purpose.

> For you created my inmost being; you knit me together in my mother's womb. I praise you because I am fearfully and wonderfully made; your works are wonderful, I know that full well. My frame was not hidden from you when I was made in the secret place, when I was woven together in the depths of the earth. Your eyes saw my unformed body; all the days ordained for me were written in your book before one of them came to be. (Psalm 139:13-16)

Yes, God has had all our days ordained; they are for good and not evil. When Satan convinces us that God is not the loving God He is, and that His mercy might extend to others but not to us, we remain the victim...and he wins.

The Great Mastermind

Satan is the greatest mastermind of all. He tries to keep us locked up in the prison of our past. Everyone makes mistakes, and, yes, sin does cast a shadow, but God is just to forgive. God wants to help us learn how to use our past mistakes as stepping stones to our future and not millstones around our neck.

When we continue to listen to the lies of the enemy, we are unable to break free. Unless we shut him out, he becomes a broken record. Remember the old phonographs? If you tried to play a record that was scratched, the needle hung up in the groove and the song skipped...and skipped...and skipped. Only when we lifted the arm and moved the needle beyond the scratch would the record be able to finish playing.

Our mind is the same way. Satan is like that broken record going around and around, skipping and skipping, repeating the same old junk. But, you see, God knows the location of every scratch in your life and my life. He knows we're not perfect, yet He offers us forgiveness. Through His unconditional love, He lifts the arm on the phonograph and moves us beyond our mistakes—beyond our scratches—and enables us to continue seamlessly in Him.

Satan *is* the father of lies. When he continues to remind us of our past, he wants us to believe we are not good enough to be who God has called us to be. He *loves* to remind us of that same old useless junk. He enjoys keeping us in the prison cell of our mind; keeping us in the cemetery of our past so we can never be free.

The apostle John tells us he comes to kill, to steal, and destroy (John 10:10). His goal is to *kill* our future, to *steal* our joy, and to *destroy* the life that God intended for us.

David's Story

Carol and I have been friends for many years. For some time, whenever we'd meet, she'd have the same request: "Please pray for David" (her son). "He's not doing good at all. The enemy has such a hold on him."

Recently, David shared his journey of victory with me over a cup of coffee.

"The enemy holds you into believing you'll never have the confidence you need to go forward," he said. "He gets you to believe your past identity, which was shattered due to failure; it's unreachable now. You begin to self-destruct into a downward spiral when you see the good of what you were, but now it seems obscure, and in no way can you see yourself becoming that again.

"It's all about identity, pride, and self-confidence," he added. "You *must* get to the point where you just cry out to God. You completely surrender your life to him and follow however He directs." Then he said—and the truth of this was such that I could see it in my own life—"The first thing God does after we surrender is to come in and heal us and our heart so we will be able to help others.

"The Lord took me to the book of Proverbs," David continued. "He helped me understand that the book of Proverbs is God's commands to us." Then David shared that one of the turning points in his life came when he saw each proverb *not* as a harsh command to crush him, but as a command to enrich his life. To follow out of love for God and what God was asking, which in turn would bring him the peace he had always wanted. When he said, "Empathy and humility with a healed heart is the key so you can go on to help others," my whole heart smiled.

His favorite verse of Scripture, he told me, is from 2 Corinthians: "Praise be to the God and Father of our Lord Jesus Christ, the Father of compassion and the God of all comfort, who comforts us in all our troubles so that we can comfort those in any trouble with the comfort we ourselves receive from God. For just as we share abundantly in the sufferings of Christ, so also our comfort abounds through Christ" (2 Cor. 1:3-5).

It's evident to see how God came in, removed the lies of the enemy, and enabled David to live his new life solely in who he is *with his identity in Christ*. This transformation has made such a dramatic impact that David is working to receive his bachelor's degree at a Christian university with the desire to bring his life-changing experiences to young adolescents. With his new identity and self-confidence in Christ, he wants to counsel and guide young teens in this unexpected journey called life.

What a joy to sit beside Carol on the other side of this experience. The mom who called out to God and with a broken heart heard Him say, "Be still and know that I am God[9]; you step out of the way and let me do my job"—oh, so difficult for her that she even pre-planned David's funeral, fearing it would happen much too soon—to a radiant mom praising God every day for the miracle she got to witness right before her eyes.

In Christ

One of my favorite games to play as a child was Monopoly. I remember when I'd pick up the "Get Out of Jail Free" card, I'd tuck it under the board *just in case* I landed in jail. I knew I had a way out.

Although sometimes I never needed it, it gave me security knowing it was there. God provides the same protection for us. He's given us over three thousand promises in the Bible, so whatever we are going through, He's got us covered.

God knew back in the garden that we'd experience times of trial. He knew that, just as Satan tempted Adam and Eve, we would also be tempted. There might be times in our life, just like in the game of Monopoly, when we begin to feel trapped with no way out. Like the other players in the game, the rest of the world goes on, but we're stuck.

God does not want us to remain in bondage. He loves us too much to let us stay there. He wants us to move out of there and to be all He's created us to be.

The minute we know who we are in Christ, we win. That is our "Get Out of Jail Free" card. We can overcome the lies and the tactics of the enemy by the blood of the Lamb and the word of our testimony.

> Since then, you have been raised with Christ, set your hearts on things above, where Christ is, seated at the right hand of God. Set your minds

on things above, not on earthly things. For you died, and your life is now hidden with Christ in God. (Colossians 3: 1-3)

Where our thoughts go, our mind will follow. Taking the time to unpack the Scripture above will keep us free. Once we have given our hearts to Jesus, and we are born into our life with Him; our old selves have *died in Christ* and now are *raised in Christ*.

That is our freedom.

And, then, whenever the enemy comes to attack, we can call out to Jesus and He will come to our rescue.

Like David reminded me over and over, peace is attainable when we turn our focus to Him. The enemy cannot barge in to attack when we bathe ourselves in the Word of God, becoming, as Colossians says, "hidden with Christ!"

Point of Victory

Satan wants us to believe we are powerless. He loves nothing more than for us to sit and sulk and believe *woe is me*—a victim's mentality. Instead of him raising a hallelujah that he's won something over on us, how much more rewarding for us to be the one raising a hallelujah that we are free.

He tries desperately to keep us believing the world is against us and we will never amount to anything. When people hurt us and treat us wrongly, he's waving a flag of victory, hoping we will fall into a pity party. He's betting we'll continue to sink lower and lower and never find our way out.

According to Webster, a victim is one who is trapped. One who is subject to oppression. Seeing ourselves as such will make us a victim. When we can begin to see ourselves fighting *from* victory instead of *for* victory, will we win the battle. Jesus already did everything we need to be free. He handed us that "Get Out of Jail Free" card when He died and shed His blood at Calvary. When we take our eyes off ourselves and turn them to Jesus, we can see freedom through His death and resurrection. This gives us everything we need to rise out of the ashes of despair. Our sins, which the enemy continually reminds us of, have been forgiven at the cross. "Since we have now been justified by his blood, how much more shall we be saved from God's wrath through him!" (Rom. 5:9).

Understanding you are justified by His blood will erase every negative word the enemy has for you. Until you fully understand what Jesus did for you, you cannot move on. Erasers remove and wipe things out. The blood of Jesus was shed to remove your sins, to wipe your sins out as far as the east is to the west.

Walking in Victory

When Jesus was in the desert, the driest place of all, Satan barged right in[10]. Being both God and man, Jesus could have given in to the tempter, but He did not. He defeated Satan *with words from the Scriptures*. He is our example. If the Word of God is powerful enough for Jesus to quote, then is it not the same for us?

The psalmist David told us the benefits of meditating on God's Word when he wrote, "Blessed is the one who does not walk in step with the wicked or stand in the way that sinners take or sit in the company of mockers, but whose delight is in the law of the LORD, and who meditates on his law day and night" (Ps. 1:1-2). When we meditate on the Word of God, we build up the arsenal we need to be able to walk in victory.

When opponents come together in battle, only one of the opponents will taste victory. One wins, one loses. We will be the one to win when we rise up in holy anger over whatever it is the enemy throws at us. We have the authority to speak to him face to face with the Word of God, as Jesus did.

Do you remember the Marvel comic superhero, the Hulk? He inspired several TV shows and movies. As a human (and scientist) he was exposed to gamma rays, which had an unusual effect on the doctor. Typically, he was mild mannered, but when he'd get angry, his chest almost exploded, the buttons on his shirt popped as fabric ripped, and he turned into a raging green monster. *Grrrrrr!*

That's how angry we need to be to walk the road of victory. To become so angry at the works of the devil, we pull our shoulders back, raise our heads, and unleash the Word of God within!

The Hulk let out his growling roar and we can do the same. Once we take the authority given in Jesus, we will be able to overcome the guilt, shame, and depression the enemy lays upon us. We must put an end to his trickery and refocus our mind on Jesus, believe the enemy is under our feet, and walk right over him and into the victorious life God has for us.

This is difficult to master. As we know, our mind will always be with us, and Satan will never give up on his attacks. But, remember that it's only when the players are on the field that the game begins. When we refuse to allow the enemy to send his players in, we have the victory!

Reflection

Take a few minutes and reflect on this chapter.

- Does Satan try to taunt you with sins from your past?
- After reading this chapter, do you believe you can be free?
- Do you understand what it means to be in Christ and risen with Him?

How will this make a difference in your life?

Meditate or journal for the Lord to equip you with what you need to experience your victory.

Memory Verse

Since then, you have been raised with Christ, set your hearts on things above, where Christ is seated at the right hand of God. Set your minds on things above, not on earthly things. For you died, and your life is now hidden with Christ in God.

(Colossians 3:1-3)

FREE IN CHRIST

Your mind is but a battlefield
where Satan loves to play.
And if he's given the access
he'll stay there every day.

But when you know the Word of God
and what the Bible says.
You'll learn to defeat every lie.
and in Jesus, move ahead.

Then when Satan tries his very best
to bury you in the past.
You will learn how to speak to him
and break out free at last.

So, meditate on the Word of God
and build your arsenal.
Then when the enemy calls you out
direct him back to hell!

THERE'S A CHANGE COMING

Not that I have already obtained all this, or have al-
ready arrived at my goal, but I press on to take hold
of that for which Christ Jesus took hold of me.
Philippians 3:12

My two sons, Michael and Brian, ran track in high
school. I'd hide under the bleachers to watch their
meets (so I wouldn't make them nervous) and stand
amazed at the speed and focus of all those young athletes. In
the relay, the first runner would run two hundred yards. He'd
pass the baton to the next runner, and this would continue to
the third and then the fourth runners. The race ended when the
fourth runner reached the finished line.

This is where we are. As we've fought, decreed and declared,
we have made it to the finish line. Now it is time to stand back
and see the glory of the Lord.

In the book of Exodus, shortly after the Israelites had left
Egypt for the promised land, we see them trapped against the
Red Sea with Pharaoh's army at their back, fearing for their lives.

> As Pharaoh approached, the Israelites looked up,
> and there were the Egyptians, marching after
> them. They were terrified and cried out to the
> LORD. They said to Moses, "Was it because there
> were no graves in Egypt that you brought us to

the desert to die? What have you done to us by bringing us out of Egypt? Didn't we say to you in Egypt, 'Leave us alone; let us serve the Egyptians'? It would have been better for us to serve the Egyptians than to die in the desert!" (Exodus 14:10-12)

Although the Israelites were slaves to Pharaoh with no lives of their own, fear of the unknown started calling them back to Egypt. Moses addressed the Israelites with power. He spoke with Godly wisdom to encourage them with the faith he had in the Lord. He said to them, "Do not be afraid. Stand firm and you will see the deliverance the LORD will bring you today. The Egyptians you see today you will never see again. The LORD will fight for you; you need only to be still" (Exod. 14:13-14).

Can you imagine what they were thinking? They could only see what was before them, and Pharaoh's army approached from behind. Fear welled up as deep as the waters stood. Moses, on the other hand, heard a specific *word* from the Lord.

Then the LORD said to Moses, "Why are you crying out to me? Tell the Israelites to move on. Raise your staff and stretch out your hand over the sea to divide the water so that the Israelites can go through the sea on dry ground. I will harden the hearts of the Egyptians so that they will go in after them. And I will gain glory through Pharaoh and all his army, through his chariots and his horsemen. The Egyptians will know that I am the LORD when I gain glory through Pharaoh, his chariots, and his horsemen." (Exodus 14:15-18).

One Word

Did God ever speak a *word* to you? Maybe others around you seemed uneasy like the Israelites, yet God used you to keep everyone else in check?

For many years we owned a business. For a few years, we tried to sell it, but each time a new prospect came, it fell through. I became weary until, one night, I had a dream. I shared it with a friend, and, through it, she believed God was telling me our property was going to sell. The evening after the dream, my husband told me his real estate agent had brought a client by that afternoon. To our surprise, they not only wanted to purchase the business, they also wanted to do so immediately—in two weeks to be exact! With the clock ticking, we had lots to do before vacating our business.

Because of the dream/word from the Lord, I, with the help of my friend Karen, continued to work tirelessly, donating items from the business to local ministries in town. Like the Israelites who had yet to see the sea part, I did not see a signature on the dotted line. But I believed it would come. My husband and brother-in-law, on the other hand, hesitated to move forward, fearing that the buyers would back out like the others in the past.

The sale day arrived. They gave us a three o'clock deadline to vacate. Finally, my husband and brother-in-law hopped on board. The dream was spot on! At 3:00 sharp, the new buyers bolted the doors closed. With a mix of tears and fears, we were on our way to an unknown future.

Once the business closed, like the Israelites, we had no choice but to move forward, believing God's hand was in this. And, as Jeremiah states: "For I know the plans I have for you, declares the LORD, plans to prosper you and not to harm you, plans to give you hope and a future" (Jer. 29:11).

And as my husband now continually reminds me, "God's still on the throne."

Humanness to Rest

Sometimes it's difficult to rest until we see our situation turn around. That is when we have to choose to remember God's last word, or promise, to us. This is when we rest in Him. He knows the beginning from the end. He would not give us a promise and renege on it. He promises to give us hope in times of an unforeseen future.

Instead of focusing on what's lurking behind, He wants us to direct our thinking to the numerous stories in the Old and New Testaments. That's where He proved faithful, where He enabled our forefathers to hear the word of the Lord and rest in Him.

Just think, if the Israelites succumbed to their feelings and did not continue to move on as Moses commanded them, they would have died sludging cement as permanent slaves of Pharaoh. And, although they walked in fear of the unknown, did God not prove faithful to them over and over?

The same with me. If I hadn't listened and believed the dream was from God, think of all the ministries that would have missed out on the blessing. Actually, the blessing went both ways—to us for being able to give, and to them for receiving.

Stand

The apostle Paul speaks to us through his own experience in Ephesians 6. He tells us to *stand*. Theologians believe Paul was nearing or in his eighties when he wrote the book of Ephesians. He was not speaking from something he read or something he learned secondhand, but from that which he had personally walked through.

In Ephesians 6:10, Paul tells us to put on the full armor "so that you can stand." Verse 13 brings us up to where we are today.

"Therefore put on the full armor of God, so that when the day of evil comes, you may be able to stand your ground, and after you have done everything, to stand." (Eph.6:13)

I recently had a dream about my son Brian. In the dream, he told me about a concert he and his fiancée were going to attend. I didn't recognize the name of the group, but I knew it was a heavy metal band. In the dream, the concert, held in a large stadium, began. As the music blared from the stage, there was a loud bang, like gunshots. Everyone panicked and ran for shelter. Brian and his fiancée were separated. Then the dream ended.

The next afternoon I received a text of a photo of my son Brian and his fiancée standing in front of a baseball stadium. I texted: "What are you guys doing at Wrigley Stadium? Baseball game?" He texted back: "Pearl Jam!"

Oh, no! That was the name of the band in my dream! I about lost it. It wouldn't have mattered so much, but many times the Lord has given me dreams, and they *do* come to true in one way or another. I called my daughter and asked her what to do. "You don't want to call him and fill them with fear," she said. "Let me be the one to call him and just to say Mom had a dream, not telling him the severity of it, but to be careful and maybe sit near the exits." Then she added, "And you do what you do best, pray."

Time for battle. I knew this was not one to fight alone. I called my friend Marty. She and I decided to do a three-way call with our friend Karen. I explained the situation, knowing that this was no coincidence! I shared everything as best I could through sobs and, yes, fear. "The very same group from my dream...Brian and Jen are in Chicago, about to see them tonight. I believe it's a warning. We must do some serious warfare."

The three of us battled for the next few hours. Whatever the Holy Spirit revealed to one, the other would either pray as a form of protection or cast down if it was not to be. Even though Karen was out of town visiting her family, she knew the urgency; she sneaked outside and joined in.

As one of us started to ask the Lord to put a shield around them, Karen busted in. "You won't believe what is in front of me!

There is a huge shield with two swords crisscrossed over it. It is gigantic on this wall right here before me."

Wow! Thank you, Lord! He allowed Karen to see something in the natural to show us He was at work in the supernatural. We warred on. Finally, the Lord said, "Praise Me."

At that same time, either Karen or Marty said, "I hear breakthrough. We need just to praise God now because the battle is won."

That evening, as the hours crawled by, I imagined minute by minute where they were until the concert ended. Although I knew God was in control, that "mom" fear would rear its head now and then. As it was with the Israelites, they had to stand and see the sea open before them. I knew as we prayed that the Lord said, "Breakthrough." But still, it was a long night.

The next day my son called while driving home. When I shared the dream, I was amazed at their response. During our prayer the night before, one of us prayed that Brian and Jen would think about their hotel room that overlooked the city of Chicago and that instead of staying at the concert, they'd decide to call it a night and go back.

After sharing the details with Brian and Jen, Jen told me, "There was one time I began to think; I've got kids at home. Is this really safe, why don't we go back to our hotel and stay there?"

Wow!

Although they didn't leave the concert, Jen shared that she no longer felt safe going to something of that magnitude again. Brian never explained why, but he repeated he knew we were praying and continued to let me know how much they appreciated the prayers.

Sometimes, even through a dream, God will call us into battle. I didn't wake up, remember the dream, and go out fighting aimlessly. It was not until I received the text "Pearl Jam!" that was my called to battle. That was my warning from the Lord to go and cover my son and his fiancée.

Even though I learned how things worked out, we do not *have* to know the outcome of our prayers. Sometimes we don't even necessarily have to know or have confirmation of whether something *is* going on, but when we get that "knowing" in our spirit, by God's Holy Spirit, our part is to pray.

Obedience is the key. God calls, and we respond, believing the outcome belongs to the Lord. When we genuinely find ourselves deep in battle, many times, but not always, we will feel a release. When Karen heard, "Breakthrough," and I heard, "Praise Me," the Holy Spirit was revealing that it was done.

God was assuring us that He had already gone ahead, and they were going to be protected. Again, our part is obedience. To take the promises in the Word of God and to pray, decree, and then stand and allow God to do the rest.

Reflection

Take a few minutes and reflect on what you just read.

- Are you a doer? Do you find it challenging to settle down and wait?
- Can you think of a time when you prayed and God said, "I've heard your prayers, now rest in Me?"
- After reading this chapter, do you think it will be easier for you next time God says to heed to His voice and wait on Him?

Meditate and allow God to give you a word to bring you to His perfect rest.

Memory Verse: Not that I have already obtained all this, or have already arrived at my goal, but I press on to take hold of that for which Christ Jesus took hold of me. (Philippians 3:12)

LET GOD BE GOD

So now that you have decreed
you have prayed and declared.
It's time for you to stand back
and know that God is there.

Know that He's heard every prayer
know He's heard every plea.
And believe in your heart, He's the one
to set the captive free.

You've prayed and released it in faith
you've laid it at the cross.
So, now's the time for God to be God
and count it, not a loss.

For if He can part the Red Sea
and zip it closed in time.
What will he do for the ones you love
and you consider as "Mine?"

CHAPTER X

WHEN IT HITS HOME

*Trust in the LORD with all your heart and lean not
on your own understanding; in all your ways submit
to him, and He will make your paths straight.*
Proverbs 3:5-6

The entire time I've worked on this book, I have encountered one battle after another. But why shouldn't I?

The first chapter of Job says that God *permitted* Satan to *test* Job's faithfulness: "The LORD said to Satan, 'Very well, then, everything he has is in your power, but on the man himself do not lay a finger'" (Job 1:12).

Some days, we all feel like Job. We all feel as if everything we have is in Satan's power and that God is sitting on the sidelines watching. And so it was with me. One morning I awoke to the ringing of my phone. "Is this Del Bates?" the lady on the other end of the line asked.

"Yes, it is," I said, my voice groggy.

I didn't understand everything she said, but I did grasp one word: *cancer.*

"*What?*" I sat straight up in bed and tried to listen attentively.

"The biopsy you had last week from the spot on your back has come back," she added. "It reveals you have a squamous cell carcinoma. It needs to be removed immediately."

As my mind traveled elsewhere, she continued with words I didn't understand. When she finished, I could hear the Lord say,

"Del, you need to rebuke every curse word that has ever been spoken against you!" It's not that I knew of any specific words anyone had spoken against me, but sometimes when we are in leadership, things may be said about us in critical manner. Since I didn't know of any specific word, I just asked that anything spoken against me would be broken in Jesus name.

I started to pray, then went to war. Although I've prayed for many others, now it was my turn. I needed to stand. I needed to pray and believe all the things I'd shared and passed on to others. Could I do it? Could I now believe that all the words of encouragement, all the warfare prayers, all the support was now available for me?

The previous evening, while I worked on this book, I knew it needed another chapter. I studied it well, and everything seemed to flow. I didn't know where to add another chapter. But, after that call, I knew. The Lord spoke loud and clear: the next chapter would be: *When It Hits Home.*

It is so easy to pray and believe for others, but now, the tables have turned, and it's time for me. Time to come against the enemy and believe for me. Time to sit with the Lord and ask Him, how do I wage this battle *for myself*?

The first thing He directed was that I was to stay off the phone. He said not to carry on with fearful conversations about what others endured because oftentimes that opens the door to fear and unbelief. We may talk to someone who says, "Oh, piece of cake! I'm praying!" Or, we may speak to someone who shares "the worst thing that can happen." Without realizing it, we put ourselves in *their* place, and fear starts to run wild.

Sometimes, instead of taking our problem or care to the Lord and trusting Him with the outcome, that's the last place we go. The apostle Peter penned it perfectly: "Cast all your anxiety on him because he cares for you" (1 Pet. 5:7).

D-Day

Surgery was scheduled for Wednesday at 8:00 a.m. I spent most of Tuesday evening listening to a sermon from my pastor, Phil Krist. He spoke just what I needed to hear: the power of your words. He said, *"Dare to declare!"* I didn't know then how crucial this word would be for me on the upcoming day.

Once my husband and I arrived at the medical office, the nurse directed us to the surgical room. The doctor joined us and gave us the plan. "First," he said, "I will remove the cancer, then I will test the margins to see that it is all removed. If the margins are clear, I will stitch the incision, and you'll be on your way. If not, I will have to go a bit deeper, remove a bit more, and go from there."

A dream from the past week flashed before me. My friend Karen said she believed that, through the dream, God was saying, "He's got your back!" I chose to believe that the dream was a word from the Lord for such a time as this.

When we ask God for help, He will be there for us. No matter what we're facing, when we seek Him, He will answer. Sometimes it's through a person, other times through His Word, and, in my case, it was through a dream. Whatever we need, He will give us a word which, in turn, will bring us peace.

After the doctor finished, he directed us to wait until he determined if the margins were clear. My husband and I held hands and prayed as we streamed worship music from my phone. I received a text from my daughter that read: "Mom, I believe that the doctor's going to be shocked. It's only going to be one incision, and you will be clear. That's what I believe God is saying will happen."

Was She Right?

About an hour later, the nurse walked in with the good news. "The cancer is clear."

After the doctor stitched the incision, he asked if I'd ever had the antibiotic Keflex, and, if so, if I'd had a reaction to it. *Interesting question,* I thought.

"No, I'm good," I answered.

After we filled the prescription, I realized that what I'd been given was not what the doctor ordered. I called the pharmacy. They assured me by explaining this was Keflex in the generic and that I'd be okay.

I started to take the medication, but for some reason, before I swallowed it, I said, "God, if there is anything in here that will hurt me, please take it out."

After I awoke from a short nap, I panicked. My back seemed to itch, and my throat felt constricted. *I could not breathe!* I called the doctor's office, and the receptionist directed me to go immediately to the nearest hospital or walk-in clinic. I called my husband. No answer. I called him again and again. Then I called my daughter. No answer. Once, twice, three times for each. *Why aren't they answering*? They always answer my call.

I cried out to the Lord. "What do I do? I can't breathe, and it's getting worse."

Just then, my husband walked in. "What's wrong?" he asked. "I can't breathe!"

With no time to waste, we rushed to the nearest clinic.

As he pulled up to the clinic, I flew out of the car, zipped through the revolving doors, and blared out, "I need help!" The two girls behind the desk rushed me back to a room.

Jesus, I prayed.

Immediately they gave me oxygen along with a shot of Benadryl and then a steroid. A doctor let me know an ambulance was on the way to take me to the hospital.

When they lifted me into the ambulance, I became afraid that I was going to die. Even though I could not get a deep enough breath, I reminded myself that I could not allow fear to take over. I *had* to believe for myself. I quoted one Scripture after another, and then I remembered a word from the pastor's sermon on Sunday. "When we don't speak in faith, we stop the hand of God from doing the miraculous!" If I wanted to be healed, I *had* to *believe* He could do it.

Although I had prayed for many others and witnessed the miraculous hand of God on so many, now it was my turn. Would the same God who helped each of them now enable me to live through this night and breathe on my own?

Our Words Are Weapons

I looked out the back window of the ambulance as I talked to God, saying, *I know I have believed for so many. I now speak to you in faith...I DO believe that you can heal me, and I will be okay.*

After those words, that very second, I breathed on my own for the first time! Thank You, Jesus! The next few hours were the usual waiting game in the emergency room. My heart continued to race because of the steroid shot, and I knew it wouldn't be safe to go home. When the doctor examined me, I told him I knew I couldn't go home. "If I do," I added, "I'll be back during the night."

He sent a tech in to draw my blood. She was anything but kind. As soon as she started, she hit a nerve. A flare of pain traveled at the speed of lightning down to my fingertips. As tears rolled down my eyes, I heard the Lord gently speak to my heart: *Thus far and no farther. You are my daughter. No one else will lay a hand on you.*

I cannot explain what happened next except to say that the Lord healed me. My heart stopped racing, the nausea went away, and I felt the same as I had twenty-four hours before.

"I want to go home," I said to my husband. "I can't explain what just happened, but I'm perfectly fine." I told him what the Lord said and that I wanted to get into my own bed.

I caught a glimpse of the doctor passing by and signaled for him. "I want to go home," I said to him.

"What? You just told me a few minutes ago you didn't think you were okay to leave."

I shared everything that happened and what the Lord had done.

"Let's wait for the results of the test," he said, "and if all is clear, you can go."

Again, I can't explain what happened in that emergency room, but I know that I had an army of warriors praying for me. My phone continued to receive texts well into the night from friends and family who were lifting me up in prayer.

Sometimes we are the ones called to battle. Other times, we are the ones to be prayed for. This is why we need one another. We need others to come to our aid and lift us up when we are down, and they need us in the same way. We can never underestimate the power of prayer.

God Does Answer Prayer

We never know what side of the battle we're going to be on. One day you might need to be the one who needs the prayer, and the very next day, you might receive the call from someone who is in need. The important thing to remember is where to go when we pray.

God is always there with an open ear to hear our prayers. But why pray if God knows everything already? If He knows the beginning from the end, *why pray*? Because this is about the strengthening of your faith. It's all about calling out to Him because He invites us to be in that intimate place with Him. "Call to me, and I will answer you and tell you great and unsearchable things you do not know" (Jer. 33:3).

Sometimes when we pray, things happen that we can't explain with logic. For instance, although the ringer on my husband's phone had been turned down (which was why he didn't hear my call), he walked in exactly when I needed him.

We may question why things happen and never get the fullness of the answers we might want to have, but through it all, He is there. He knows our hearts, our needs, and He is more than ready to keep us in His perfect peace. He is a supernatural God, and when we *expect* the supernatural and believe it is possible, that is what unties His hands to move.

God longs to do things we can't even imagine. Daily we endure stressful situations. God desires to lift us out of the tough spots we're in, even if it's in a supernatural way, in order to reveal His power.

I pray that you remember, when it hits home for you, *He will be there!*

Reflection
Take a few minutes and reflect on what you just read.

- What "battle" has hit home for you?
- Do you believe God is there to help you through?
- Can you trust that if He can help others, He will carry you?

Meditate or journal and ask the Lord to help you walk in faith and weigh your words carefully.

Memory Verse
*Trust in the LORD with all your heart and lean not
on your own understanding;
in all your ways submit to him, and He will make
your paths straight.*
Proverbs 3:5-6

ONLY BELIEVE

We never know what side of the battle
we will be on each day.
We never know if for "me" or "you,"
we will have to pray.

For if the battle is for you
it's easier you see.
Cuz I can stand and just believe
God will be all you need.

But oh my gosh, if it's for me
it's another thing you know.
For then I have to fully trust
what I've told others and so.

So, since our life's but a mystery
from one day to the next.
Trust in the Lord with all your heart
and you'll have no regret!

CHAPTER XI

VICTORY IN THE BATTLE

Let us not become weary in doing good, for at the
proper time we will reap a harvest if we do not give
up.
Galatians 6:9

There's nothing like the birth of a baby. The new mom-to-be pushes, cries, and she might even belt out an unexpected scream, but she gets through the pain as God gives her the strength to go on. Then...the joy! The unspeakable joy as this precious new life enters the world. The new mother can breathe a sigh of relief.

Although the pain may be intense, every mother knows the joy that follows. As we go forth with our battle plan for prayer, we may feel like that laboring mom at times, but we expect and know the joy that follows.

Sometimes when we are praying for victory, we might see an instant result—a quick delivery—but then other results are like some labors, filled with hours and hours of pain.

My son Michael frequently travels for work. As I was deleting some of his old texts from my phone, I had to laugh. Every text he sent was either, "Boarding, pray," or, "Thanks, landed." In those times, the time frame for prayer might be an hour or two. So yes, I prayed as he asked, and many times, when the Holy Spirit prompted, I even prayed while he was in mid-air, especially in bad weather.

But then, unlike those seamless or turbulent flights, there are the times when it seems our answers never come. There are times when we contend and continue to pray for a loved one who has backslidden—someone who walked close to the Lord for a time, but who, for whatever reason, has fallen away and is following the ways of the world instead of God. We pray and believe, but nothing happens; we are not seeing the fruit of our labor. Sometimes we even begin to think that God is not hearing our prayers. We call out to Him and ask if He's forgotten us.

Other times we may pray for someone with a troubled marriage. We may believe separation is not the answer and we keep believing for them, but we don't see one or the other budging from their stubborn behavior.

My word to you today is: Do *not* give up! God *is* hearing those prayers and victory *is* on the way. In the story found in the Old Testament book of Daniel, Daniel, who had been taken into captivity by the Babylonian king Nebuchadnezzar, mourned and prayed over what happened to the city of his birth, Jerusalem.

Daniel knew God, and he did not blame God for his people's exile because he knew and understood that the people, as a whole, had turned their backs on God and had inflicted God's punishment on themselves. Eventually, Babylon fell to Persia and Daniel with it. But instead of throwing in the towel, Daniel turned to God in prayer: "At that time, I, Daniel, mourned for three weeks. I ate no choice food; no meat or wine touched my lips; and I used no lotions at all until the three weeks were over" (Dan. 10:2-3). Daniel persisted until his answer arrived.

> On the twenty-fourth day of the first month, as I was standing on the bank of the great river, the Tigris, I looked up and there before me was a man dressed in linen, with a belt of fine gold from Uphaz around his waist. His body was like topaz, his face like lightning, his eyes like flaming torch-

es, his arms and legs like the gleam of burnished
bronze, and his voice like the sound of a multi-
tude. I, Daniel, was the only one who saw the vision; those who were with me did not see it, but
such terror overwhelmed them that they fled and
hid themselves. (Daniel 10:4-7)

Re-read the last line. There were others with Daniel, *but they
fled, in fear amd terror.* To be honest, I might have done the same
thing. But Daniel, filled with *holy fear,* stood trembling, then fell
to his knees.

God *had* heard Daniel's prayers; through the words of the angel, Daniel learned why his prayers weren't answered *immediately,* as he had surely hoped they would be.

Then he continued, "Don't be afraid, Daniel. Since
the first day that you set your mind to gain understanding and to humble yourself before your
God, your words were heard, and I have come in
response to them. But the prince of the Persian
kingdom resisted me twenty-one days. Then Michael, one of the chief princes, came to help me,
because I was detained there with the king of Persia. (Daniel 10:12-13)

Somctimes we get to see what the hold up is, and other times
we do not. Daniel had not given up, even though he might have
felt time was of the essence. Scripture tells us that he was about
eighty years old at the time of this vision. But regardless of his
age, persistence paid off.

Although we can't see what is going on in the heavenly realm,
we understand from Scripture that the forces of evil hindered
Daniel's answer. Many times, it is the same with us. Yet, hearing

the angel's reply assures us that God is always working behind the scenes.

Go the Extra Mile

Following in Daniel's footsteps, we can see that persistence pays off. Fasting was also a part of Daniel's prayer. If the Lord calls us to a fast, He does so to get our complete attention. When we let go of our fleshly desires and choose to give up individual needs or wants to hear the Lord more clearly, He will speak to us.

Fasting was not only for the Old Testament. God may call us to a fast to make room and time for Him, and He honors our fasting when we abstain from certain foods for a while. Although it might be difficult when you begin, the longer you pursue, the easier it gets.

Sometimes we might be expecting God to move in one direction, then out of the blue, everything changes. We never, ever know. He is sovereign, and when we surrender all, like Daniel, with prayer and fasting, God will show up—but not always on our timetable. Even if we can't see the results when contending for a situation, if we hold on long enough, like the mother in labor, we will soon see the victory come to pass.

Get God out of the Box

If we really want to see our prayers answered, we need to get God out of the box. The key is knowing that He is God and that He sees the more excellent way. He sees into the natural realm as well as the spiritual. Isaiah 55 confirms that His ways are higher than our ways.[11]

By taking God out of the box, we untie His hands to perform the miracles we want to see. We allow Him to do what only He can. With our finite minds, we can only imagine our prayers being answered in a certain way. But because God is infinite, He has resources we can't even imagine to bring victory beyond our wildest dreams.

As I shared previously, years ago, we owned a business. It was not *just* a business; it was a hotel and a place of ministry for the Lord. Over a period of time, we had the property on the market. I believed in my heart that the one who purchased it would continue to use it for the Lord.

For a season, we had numerous prospects search it out. When someone came in with the idea to tear it down, I'd cringe. I had God in this box because I wanted the next person who owned it to run it as a Christian hotel, just like we had. I'd get so excited if the potential buyers were strong Christians with a flourishing ministry and I'd think they were the ones!

Over and over, the same scenario played out. Our agent would bring in a possible buyer; I'd search them out on the internet and wait for the outcome.

Then one Sunday, I returned home from a writing conference to find my husband had something to share. "Well," he started. "This is it. Our agent brought someone by, and they want the hotel. They also want to close in thirteen days."

It was all spelled out in one breath. Nothing matched up. My husband gave me all the details, but nothing fell into place. They were *not* Christians, and they were *not* going to continue the hotel as a place for the Lord. Instead—*condos*? Yes, they planned to tear it down and put up oceanside condos.

How could this be? It didn't fit *my* plan or what I believed the Lord had told me. I was devastated. I felt like Daniel, wondering if God had heard my prayer all along.

It wasn't until about four years after the sale that He allowed me to see the full picture. We didn't need to be in *that* building to do kingdom work. God had released us by freeing us from the chains of being tied to a business 24/7. This became a blessing in disguise, although we couldn't see it originally. God's work in us and through us was not bound *just* to that hotel building.

The Victory

The victory is His. Five years ago, I could have never seen our property being demolished as a victory. Or condos standing on the property I always referred to as "holy ground." But *God* knew the future. He knew what I could not know and saw what I could not see. He is the waymaker, and He always goes before us. For that, we must continue to pray, "Thy will be done, on earth as it is in heaven."[12]

Then, when we see the tables turning and things beginning to happen that are not according to our plan, no matter how difficult it may be, we must move aside and let Him out of the box, allowing Him to make the moves as only He can.

Just like the mom ready to deliver her baby, she may not know the pain she will go through, but she does know the outcome. If we are prepared to battle every battle the same way, even though we do not see the result, we will be able to walk in peace as His plan unfolds.

Resurrected Life

We can't give up on our prayers or dreams. The worst thing we can do is allow what God has put on our hearts to die just because things may not be going our way or on our timetable.

The disciples had to be heartbroken beyond anything we can imagine with the crucifixion and death of their beloved leader and teacher Jesus. But had He not tried to tell them? Had He not tried to prepare them for things to come? How, then, could they have not understood?

Do not let your hearts be troubled. You believe in God; believe also in me. My Father's house has many rooms; if that were not so, would I have told you that I am going there to prepare a place for you? And if I go and prepare a place for you I will come back and take you to be with me that you also may be where I am. (John 14:1-3)

In this section of Scripture, we see Jesus preparing His disciples because the time of His death was coming soon. They didn't know and couldn't have known, but Jesus did. He knew what He was about to suffer, only hours away.

Before long, the world will not see me anymore, but you will see me. Because I live, you also will live. On that day you will realize that I am in my Father, and you are in me, and I am in you. (John 14:19-20)

Jesus was giving them a promise that even if they could not see Him, they would be able to continue on with His ministry as they had when He lived with them. He was letting them know that even though He would not be *in view*, the Holy Spirit living inside of them would enable them to go on without Him.

Jesus gives us the same promises. He lets us know that although situations happen and turn our world upside down, He is still there. And when we least expect it, He will show himself strong, just as He did to the disciples.

On the evening of that first day of the week, when the disciples were together, with the doors locked for fear of the Jewish leaders, Jesus came and stood among them and said, "Peace be with you!" (John 20:19)

Jesus knew the disciples were troubled. As they hid behind closed doors, He came to bring them peace. He appeared supernaturally to calm their fears and complete the promise He had given them before He died—that they *would* see Him again.

So, as we go forward, like that expectant mom in labor, or Daniel crying out for his beloved city Jerusalem, or even the fearful disciples of Jesus, let us remember that God is aware of our prayers and will answer them—all in His power. As with the disciples, He will give us His peace.

Reflection
Take a few minutes and reflect on what you just read.

- Have you been praying for a specific situation?
- Does it ever seem like God is not answering?
- After reading this chapter, can you renew your trust and know that He hears your prayer?

Meditate and allow God to speak to your heart, reassuring you that He is there.

Memory Verse

Let us not become weary in doing good, for at the proper time we will reap a harvest if we do not give up. Galatians 6:9

V-I-C-T-O-R-Y

*There is victory in the battle
it's time for you to see.
There's victory in the battle
against the enemy.*

*Don't give up on unanswered prayer
if it's not said and done.
Continue on—persist and pray
until the battle's won.*

*Believe that God has heard your prayer
He's heard your every plea.
And He will send an army in
to defeat the enemy.*

*So don't give up on prayers, my friend
stand firm in faith today.
And when you take God out of the box
He'll answer your prayer—His way!*

CHAPTER XII

SHOW ME YOUR GLORY

*And the L*ORD *said to Moses, "I will do the very thing you have asked, because I am pleased with you and I know you by name." Then Moses said, "Now show me your glory."*
Exodus 33:17-18

Moses questioned God. Have you ever wondered if it was wrong of Moses to do that? He had been face-to-face with God and had led the Israelites as God commanded. He was a faithful servant and continued to do everything God asked. But then, after all that, Moses questioned God.

Have you ever been there? You knew God called you to be an intercessor for a family member or friend and you answered the call. Daily you prayed on their behalf, and yet you saw no change. And then—you paused. You became a bit like Moses.

> Moses said to the LORD, "You have been telling me, 'Lead these people,' but you have not let me know whom you will send with me. You have said, 'I know you by name and you have found favor with me.' If you are pleased with me, teach me your ways, so I may know you and continue to find favor with you. Remember that this nation is your people." (Exodus 33:12-13)

Did you catch that? Moses is reminding God that this nation is *His* people. A bit funny, don't you think? Like, God, they're not *my* people, they're *yours!*

This conversation took place between God and Moses after Moses returned from Mt. Sinai. He had been there for forty days and nights; God gave him the Ten Commandments, directions to construct the tabernacle, and directions on how to worship God properly. His return from the mountain was far from what Moses expected; it was not a sound of victory.

> When the people saw that Moses was so long in coming down from the mountain, they gathered around Aaron and said, "Come, make us gods who will go before us. As for this fellow Moses, who brought us up out of Egypt, we don't know what has happened to him.' Aaron answered them, "Take off the gold earrings that your wives, your sons, and your daughters are wearing, and bring them to me." So, all the people took off their earrings and brought them to Aaron. He took what they handed him and made it into an idol cast in the shape of a calf, fashioning it with a tool. Then they said, "These are your gods, Israel, who brought you up out of Egypt." (Exodus 32:1-4)

Because of their sin, God told Moses to go ahead to the land He promised to give them, but that He would not go with them because they were "a stiff-necked people."

Can you see how Moses would have been frustrated and beside himself? He had been on Mt. Sinai receiving direction from God on how to lead His people, and in their impatience, they sinned and constructed a false god. Then, because of the anger burning within Him, God told Moses He would not go with them into the promised land.

When we continue to pray for someone and they remain stiff-necked, we can become as frustrated as Moses. You may even be ready to give them over to God and say, "They're *yours*; what more can I do?"

However, although Moses was frustrated, he did not give up. He wanted to continue to be a servant for the LORD. When he asked God to teach him his ways, the LORD replied, "My Presence will go with you, and I will give you rest" (Exod. 33:14).

We must do the same. We need to press on, asking God to teach us and to give us revelation of how to continue to minister to someone who keeps going around the same old mountain.

My husband Jon is involved with prison ministry. Throughout the years, he's ministered to many of the male prisoners. Over and over again he's experienced the heartbreak of praying for someone who is released back into society, and in no time, they end up returning to incarceration.

> One man in particular comes to mind. Cliff, (not his real name) is the perfect example. Although he loved the Lord, Cliff had a severe addiction problem. My husband went to the jail, ministered to Cliff, and helped him toward a release. When Cliff was released, he believed in his heart he'd never return.

> One evening we heard a knock on our door. It was Cliff and his wife. They wanted to pray with us and to thank us for what God had done. They were so grateful and convinced that this was the end of the merry-go-round in their marriage. Together, we prayed wholeheartedly in agreement.

> Sadly, a few months later, that unwanted phone call came. Cliff was back in, and he was calling on

my husband to come see him. As tough as it was for my husband, he dropped what he was doing and went.

Although Jon was frustrated and disappointed (like Moses), he did visit Cliff. He prayed with him and believed for the best. Then...prayers were answered in the way we'd hoped. Now, ten years later at the time of this writing, Cliff is still with his wife, clean and following the Lord. He is also an elder in his church.

God used what looked like an impossible situation for His glory. That is why we need to be like Moses: even if we can't see someone changing, we must continue to pray and leave the results to God.

There is nothing like seeing the glory of God—in prayer or in worship. Whenever we call, God does show up.

Let His Glory Fall

Although it's not something we can physically describe to another, God desires to manifest His glory to us. He has a way of touching us with His presence that words cannot explain.

And when we feel it, we operate in it, knowing that this is how God reveals himself to us—just like with Moses, who went up the mountain a second time to receive the new set of stone tablets (in righteous anger he had destroyed the first set). Moses could have simply sneaked off to corner and asked God for a new set of tablets. But, out of obedience, he traveled up that mountain one more time.

We typically have it a little easier; we may pray in our prayer room or get on a prayer call. Moses had quite a journey to have this next encounter with God, but oh, how worth it this trip was!

Scripture says that when he came down from being with God, his face was radiant, and the people were afraid to come near him.[13]

Imagine that! Imagine being so intimate with the Lord in prayer that His glory overtakes us, so that when we walk out of our prayer time, anyone who lays eyes on us will know we have been in the presence of Almighty God.

That is His glory! That is what He has for you. That is what He has for me. He wants to remove us so far from ourselves as we humbly enter into His presence that we quietly sit and hear what only He has to say.

Little do many people know, quietness in His presence is a form of warfare. The enemy cannot come near us and attack our mind if our eyes and focus are set firmly on the Lord.

Holy Ground

When family and friends stop by for a visit, what is the first thing they do when they enter? In our home, they remove their shoes.

We don't need a sign that says, *Please remove your shoes.* Most people, out of courtesy or respect, simply remove their shoes. But, do you know the reason for this gesture in biblical times?

The significance of removing one's shoes is a sign of submission...a way of giving up your rights. When Moses first encountered God at the burning bush on Mount Horeb, the Lord called out to Moses, who replied, "Here I am."

> "Do not come any closer," God said. "Take off your sandals, for the place where you stand is holy ground." (Exodus 3:4-5)

By telling Moses to remove his sandals, God was telling him to submit, to give up his rights and authority, and to walk in God's authority. God had big plans for Moses's life, and He has big plans for you and me. We, like Moses, have a choice: to submit to God's authority or to go our own way.

Thank God Moses submitted to His will.

One of the plans God had for Moses was to set up the tabernacle, a sanctuary where God would dwell, and where the priests would come once a year to make atonement for the sins of all.

The tabernacle was constructed with an inner and an outer court. The high priest was the only one allowed in the inner court—often referred to as the holy of holies—which was separated by a veil sewn in royal colors.

Within this holy place, no words were spoken except by God. The priests had special garments made with bells sewn on the bottom, so if at any time the bells stopped ringing, the person worshiping in the outer courts would know that the priest inside had died from being in the presence of a holy God without first being purified. And, because only the high priest could enter into the holy of holies, he would have to be pulled out by the rope tied around his waist. This sounds intimidating, doesn't it? *But,* when Jesus died, everything changed for all!

> And when Jesus had cried out again in a loud voice, he gave up his spirit. At that moment the curtain of the temple was torn in two from top to bottom. The earth shook, the rocks split... (Matthew 27:50-51)

The veil separated man from God. Through Jesus's death on the cross, we now have access to the "holy place."

The writer of Hebrews explains the access we now have to the Father.

> Therefore, brothers and sisters, since we have confidence to enter the Most Holy Place by the blood of Jesus, by a new and living way opened for us through the curtain, that is, his body, and since we have a great priest over the house of God, let

us draw near to God with a sincere heart and with the full assurance that faith brings, having our hearts sprinkled to cleanse us from a guilty conscience and having our bodies washed with pure water. (Hebrews 10:19-22)

Yes, we now have access to the Father. We may enter into that secret place where only the priests could dwell. We can come boldly into the holy of holies, and we can enter in by the blood of the Lamb!

Access to the Holy of Holies

When I was a child, we'd go to my grandparents' house to visit. We had full run of the house, except...we were never allowed to go into their bedroom. I recall standing in the hall to peek in, but I was never to step foot over the threshold.

One day I asked Grandma why we could go anywhere in the house, but not her bedroom. "It's a Grandpa and Grandma place," she whispered in her thick Italian accent. Although I didn't understand it then, I honored her wish. Then, one day, she took me by the hand and let me go into her bedroom. My grandfather was near the end of his life; I can still remember the fear I felt as I walked in.

But the love I felt as Grandpa extended his hand released that fear and drew me to his side. The love God has for us is, to a greater extent, is seen through the death of His Son, Jesus. The curtain that once separated us from God is now open. We do not have to wait for the high priest to forgive our sins on the Day of Atonement (still observed by Jews today as Yom Kippur). We have access on any given day to enter into the holy of holies to have open communication with our heavenly Father.

Take note: this is the one thing the enemy does *not* want us ever to understand!

God wants our fellowship. He wants intimacy. When we come into that quiet place with Him, we can release all that weighs heavily on our minds. When we sit in silence before Him, it's His opportunity to reveal the strategies we need for the day ahead, for every battle we will face. When we shut the world out, it allows God to move in. This is His desire.

But Satan knows that when we give a few moments to God, it can change our entire outlook on any significant battle or decision before us. He knows this is a weapon of warfare. He knows that quietness with Him leads to our knowing how to thwart the plans of the enemy. Satan does not like it, which is all the more reason for us to yearn for it!

So what are you waiting for? Be like Moses. Escape to your Mount Sinai. Though your journey might not be quite as intense as Moses's, take time to be alone. Remove your sandals and enter into the holy of holies.

Reflection

Take a few minutes and reflect on what you just read.

- Do you see how Moses could have been upset with God?
- Have you ever been there? What did you do? Say?
- When was the last time you visited your "Mt. Sinai"?

Meditate or journal, and as you sit quietly with the Lord, jot down whatever He has to say to you.

Memory Verse

And the LORD said to Moses, "I will do the very thing you have asked, because I am pleased with you, and I know you by name." Then Moses said, "Now show me your glory." (Exodus 33:17-18)

HOLY GROUND

We long to see Your Glory Lord
as Moses did that day.
Oh, how we long to see Your glory
as we come to pray.

We come in humble adoration
we bow before Your throne.
The Lord of Lords, the King of Kings
My God—it's You alone.

We come into that secret place
to seek the great "I AM."
Entering by the precious blood
precious blood of the lamb.

We leave the world so far behind
and humbly come to You.
To clear our mind and heal our heart
as only You can do!

CHAPTER XIII

THE THREE Ps: PRAISE, PRAISE, AND MORE PRAISE

*Let everything that has breath praise the L*ORD.
Psalm 150:6

My mom loved music. Her love instilled a similar love in me and each of my siblings, even to today.

I loved our Friday evening dance sessions. Mom would move our small kitchen table over to one wall, then she'd slide the dining room table to the other. In the blink of an eye, our everyday kitchen was transformed into a glorious dance floor.

Mom's greatest loves were stage plays and musicals, and one of her favorites was *The King and I*. As the music started to play on the old stereo, she'd take turns dancing with each of us, gliding us gracefully across the floor.

Sometimes we'd get impatient waiting for our turn, so we'd begin to dance with one another—what a joyous memory of how that little bungalow lit up when the music flooded our home! As my mom danced and I visualized Yul Brynner and Deborah Kerr waltzing across the floor, my mind cleared of any cares I had.

Worship Sets the Stage
God desires the same for us. As my mom pushed the table aside to make room for us to dance, God loves nothing more than when we push our worldly cares aside to make room to worship Him.

When we enter into that place of worship, be it at home, church, or a time of prayer, His presence becomes a glory cloud above us.

That's the power of worship. It releases all the cares of the world so we can totally focus on God. Once we enter in and meditate on the words we are singing, we experience a deeper level of who He is. As we talked about in the last chapter, it's like entering into the holy of holies.

Worship sets the stage for the most potent warfare there is. Some commentaries suggest that before Satan was cast out of heaven, his position was head of worship. He was created as one of the most beautiful angels. The fact that he refused to worship God and wanted to be higher than Him, and the thought of us worshiping the God he despises, turns him completely away; he cannot stand to hear our praises!

Old Testament Worshipers Lead the Way

We can learn so much about worship from the Old Testament. In 2 Chronicles 20, we see King Jehoshaphat in a dire situation. A vast army was coming against him. All the people were afraid; they feared for their lives. But look at what he did and how helpful this can be to us when we are in fear.

> Alarmed, Jehoshaphat resolved to inquire of the LORD, and he proclaimed a fast for all Judah. The people of Judah came together to seek help from the LORD; indeed, they came from every town in Judah to seek him. (2 Chronicles 20:3-4)

As they fasted and cried out to the Lord for help, God let them know He heard their prayer. He will do the same for us. In their situation, God sent a prophet who stood amongst them with a message of hope. He does the same for us. Sometimes the message comes from a friend, or maybe a devotion we read, or even the words of a song during worship. But He always lets us know He's listening, and He always brings us a word of comfort or wisdom.

> This is what the LORD says to you: "Do not be afraid or discouraged because of this vast army. For the battle is not yours, but God's." (v. 15)

After this word of encouragement, Jehoshaphat told them to have faith and how to proceed in their battle.

> After consulting the people, Jehoshaphat appointed men to sing to the LORD and to praise Him for the splendor of His holiness as they went out at the head of the army, saying: "Give thanks to the LORD, for His love endures forever." (v. 21)

It's interesting to see what God did as they started to praise Him.

> As they began to sing and praise, the LORD set ambushes against the men of Ammon and Moab and Mount Seir who were invading Judah, and they were defeated. The Ammonites and Moabites rose up against the men from Mount Seir to destroy and annihilate them. After they finished slaughtering the men from Seir, they helped to destroy one another. (v. 22)

Imagine that! They praised God, and He sent ambushes against their enemies! They obeyed the word of the Lord to send those who worshiped God first, and God did His part. The Lord will do the same for us. When we start our battle in praise and thanksgiving for all He has done, He will move heaven and earth on our behalf. Only when we understand how vital praise *is* will we see it as one of the weapons of our warfare.

How Do We Get There?

So, if you're new to worship, how do you get there? And what do you do once you're there?

I remember my first experience with worship. Coming from a denominational church, I didn't "get it." A friend, Jan, brought me to a spirit-filled church; I was like a fish out of water. Drums, keyboard, and guitars had me ready to run for the door. The service was like a jam session. Singing. Raising hands. Praising God. I was so full of hurt at the time that all I wanted was for someone to notice me and let me know that everything was going to be okay. Instead, they seemed to be into themselves and what they were doing; I felt so left out.

Now, twenty-five-plus years later, I not only "get it," I want *you* to experience it, too. When we face problems and feel completely alone, those are the times to put on worship music and *get alone with God*. Or, if you are in church and it is a time of worship, enter in. Don't be a *spectator*; be a *participator*. There's no need to worry about what others do around us. Just let go of yourself, enter in, and allow the Holy Spirit of God to overtake you and minister to your deepest needs. Although it may seem uncomfortable at first, don't think about others who may be watching. This is about you and God.

Throughout Scripture, God calls us to come and worship Him.

> Praise ye the LORD. Praise God in his sanctuary: praise him in the firmament of his power. Praise him for his mighty acts: praise him according to his excellent greatness. Praise him with the sound of the trumpet: praise him with the psaltery and harp. Praise him with the timbrel and dance: praise

him with stringed instruments and organs.
Praise him upon the loud cymbals: praise
him upon the high sounding cymbals.
Let everything that hath breath praise the LORD.
Praise ye the LORD. (Psalm 150:1-6 KJV)

These verses give praise to God for Who He is, what He has done, and in the manner He desires.

Worship songs are created to draw us into God's presence and to tell Him how much we love Him; a time of allowing us to forget who we are, and to humbly let the Holy Spirit take over.

A Time to War

And then...then there is a time "to war." Certain songs draw us into the presence of God, but others call us to prepare for battle. To fight. To war! One of my favorites is "I Raise a Hallelujah" (by Jonathan David Helser, Melissa Helser, Molly Skaggs, Raquel Vega). The words proclaim what we need to do, which is to raise a halleluiah in the presence of the enemy, knowing that heaven will come and fight for us! That is a call to war. That is a call to battle.

That is a call not merely to mouth words, but to get them into our spirit. To know that we are proclaiming powerful words from our mouth; that we do raise a hallelujah, which means "praise ye" (the Lord), in the midst of whatever is going on; and that even if everything seems bleak and we have no way out, we are going to praise God, stand on His Word, and know that as we praise, He is going to work in the middle of the storm.

Songs are not *just* pieces of music. These specific songs are a battle cry unto the Lord. It's like the musicals we listened to as kids. They told a story. They had a purpose, and as we heard the words, we followed the lives and the relationships of the characters. We became part of the songs. Worship is the same. We sing the words and prophetically we make declarations to the enemy of what will be.

We take our stance that we know the Lord has given, and then we clear everything away, just as my mom did in our kitchen.

Reflection

Take a few minutes and reflect on this chapter.

- How do you see worship?
- Do you have a clear understanding of worship and its significance?
- After reading this chapter, can you now see how worship is a weapon?

Meditate or journal and ask the Lord to give you a victory chant today.

Memory Verse

> *Let everything that has breath praise the LORD.*
> Psalm 150:6

PRAISE IS MY WEAPON

When you see praise as a weapon
you'll enter with a shout.
When you see praise as a weapon
you'll kick the enemy out.

You'll walk in with a knowing
God's there behind the scene.
And you'll come out then praising
as joy will supersede.

He's the One who holds your future
In the palm of His hand.
The One who knows your every need
and everything you've planned.

So praise Him, praise Him, praise Him
Give Him the glory due.
Trusting he has he the right answer
to give today to you!

CHAPTER XIV

WHEN YOU NEED TO GO IN ALONE

Have I not commanded you? Be strong and coura-
geous. Do not be afraid; do not be discouraged, for
the LORD your God will be with you wherever you
go.
Joshua 1:9

"**F**or where two or three gather in my name, there am
I with them" (Matt. 18:20). Yes, that is what Jesus
tells us, but what if there are not two or three? What
if there is only one? Is Jesus still there?

It's so easy for us to believe that if we have a problem, someone will always be there to join us in the battle. Someone to pray
with or agree with, or someone to hear what the Spirit is saying.

But what if...just what if...no one is there in our time of need.
Either we call upon others and they do not answer, or they are
not available when we need them most. What do we do?

Florida, like any other state, has its good and bad points. Many
refer to it as the Sunshine State, but wait until hurricane season
rolls around; most people scoot! In 2004 the whole state was hit
by four hurricanes; the east coast of Florida was hit by two of
those major category hurricanes within three weeks.

When Frances, the first one to directly hit Florida's east
coast, came barreling straight for our coastal city, my husband

suggested that my friend Diana and I head to St Augustine, about four hours north. We arrived late at night to a hotel filled with other hurricane runaways.

Although Dianna and I prayed, warred, and decreed all night long, the storm battered our town of Vero Beach clear through the next day. Swell after swell, along with devastating tornados, pounded our coast, leaving massive damage. Power outages and destruction blanketed our city. My husband was aware of my asthmatic condition and suggested that I not return until power was restored and things were cleaned up. Diana and I decided to follow one another and travel to our hometowns; Diana was from Canada while my home state is Michigan. That was the plan... until...

...until we reached the border of South Carolina, where Diana signaled to pull over. For some reason, I knew in my spirit when I pulled up behind her that she would run back to my car and say "I'm going back."

"What? I can't travel to Michigan alone," I said. "I've never driven by myself...and with all the rains...I can't do it." I almost begged her not to turn around, but her mind was made up.

Next thing I knew, I was back on the freeway *alone.* Was I scared? Absolutely! Although I knew I had the Lord, there was a fear in me like never before.

I drove most of the day, then stopped in North Carolina for the night. Morning came. I decided to get up early and drive on. Then, not too far into my trip... *fog*! And, along with the fog, a light drizzle, making matters worse for my journey as I drove through the mountains.

I called my husband for an update and my nephew answered. "Part of the hotel's roof was blown off yesterday. Uncle Jon is up there trying to secure it best he can. I guess you and Abby" (my six-week-old puppy—did I mention her?) "are on your own."

I knew I had prayer partners, but how could I talk *and* concentrate on this treacherous road? With white knuckles, a wing and a prayer, I went on.

I turned on the radio for a weather update but caught a well-known preacher starting his morning broadcast instead. "When you're in a storm," he began, "God will always see you through." And to really get my attention, he added that if the fog is too dense for you to see through, remember God is right there to shine His light in the midst.

Although I wanted two or three to pray with me, I knew that, better still, I had the Father, Son, and the Holy Spirit—that's all I needed! As the pastor's sermon ended, the fog lifted. I drove through a tunnel in West Virginia. As the nose of my car peeked out, I squinted and blinked. Sunshine! Just like the preacher said.

Alone

So, what will you do if no one is there? Imagine if your worst fear ever happened, and, at the same time, all of our nation's grids were attacked, cutting off all communication? What if you couldn't reach your loved ones and they couldn't contact you?

We must know how to call out to God on our own. As the Scripture at the beginning of this chapter reminds us, Jesus is "in the midst." But we must be assured that we know, beyond a shadow of a doubt, that even if we do not have two or three, He is always there for us.

I didn't have Diana, or my husband, or even one prayer partner. I had to rely on God alone. Turns out, He was all I had and all I needed.

Seek Him in Plenty; He'll Be There in the Drought

Psalm 105 says, "Look to the Lord and his strength; seek his face always" (Ps. 105:4). Our part is to stay in the Word, and, like the Scripture says, to seek Him. When we discover what the Bible has to say, then, when we do face unforeseen circumstances in our lives, He will be as close as our own breath. Discovering Who He is and the many facets of His character is the key.

Three weeks after Frances hit, a second hurricane, Jeanne, barreled in. Jeanne caused significant additional damage. In the aftermath, with devastation everywhere, I thought God had abandoned us. *How could He do this when we just finished such major remodeling throughout the entire hotel,* I wondered.

About three weeks after the storms, I returned from Michigan. My heart was broken. Slowly I made my way down the hall, where I could see paint stripped off the walls. Our beautiful restaurant overlooking the ocean, once encased in glass on all three sides, was reduced to a platform with heaps of sand everywhere.

In my disbelief and feelings of abandonment, I decided to go to my favorite hangout, Room 400, which overlooked the ocean and, in the past, had given me peace. I grabbed a notebook and asked God to help me understand why. Why had He allowed all of this to happen? I sat and waited until He responded with words that startled me: "I am sovereign. I rain on the just and the unjust."[14] Although at that time I didn't know the exact "address," I knew it was Scripture.

And I knew very well what He was saying. Many times, when category three or four hurricanes threatened to make landfall on our coast, God through His grace and mercy *had* spared us. But for whatever reason, and we'll probably never know on this side of eternity, He let these two hurricanes rip right through.

Although we've learned throughout this book how to war, how to decree and how to declare when the battle rages and the enemy sets traps before us, we must remember that God is sovereign. He still and always will have the *last* say. We may not like the outcome, but no matter what, we must leave it to Him.

Sometimes when we pray, expect things to go our way, and they don't, the first thing we do is blame the enemy. I think we give him way more credit than he deserves. With the answer I received from the Lord, I knew it was not about blaming Satan.

There are times unbeknownst to us when God *allows* bad things to happen. As difficult as it is, we need to try and move on, to pick up the pieces, and to let God be God and do it His way. When we take the good and the bad, the explainable and the un-explainable, we experience a sense of peace in the midst of any storm that comes our way.

So, yes, maybe there *will* be times when no one is there as you reach out for another voice, another hand. That is where you take hold of what you've gleaned from the past, what you've learned from Scripture, and what the Holy Spirit has taught you.

You *stand.*

Reflection
Take a few minutes and reflect on this chapter.

- Have you ever had a time when it was just you and God?
- Do you have a relationship with God such that if you could not reach anyone, you'd feel close enough to call on Him?
- If you don't have that close relationship with Him, why not call upon Him today? He's waiting.

Meditate or journal for the Lord to equip you with what you need in order to experience your victory.

Memory Verse:
> *Do not be afraid; do not be discouraged, for*
> *the Lord your God will be with you wherever you*
> *go.*
> Joshua 1:9

WHAT IF

What if the time should ever come
when you have to pray alone?
What if the time should ever come
when you can't get to a phone?
What if one time you needed to pray
and no one to pray with you?
Do you believe you'd be at peace
and God would help you through?
We hope that would never be the case
and access would be there.
That we'd always have another
to join us in a prayer.
But just in case it did per se
God wants you to know.
That He will be just a word away
And He'll never let you go!

ABOUT THE AUTHOR

Del Bates is an author, speaker, and an enthusiastic encouragement to many.

She is the president of Treasure Coast Word Weavers and Assistant to the Florida State Leader, Sherry Anderson in Aglow Int.

She has self-published two books and has numerous stories in various publications. She and her husband, Jon, are snowbirds between Florida and Michigan. Besides having a heart for prayer and the Lord, she finds her peace with with three grown children, their families, and her five precious grandchildren.

Her heart's desire is to further the Kingdom of God through her *Pen For the Lord*.

To contact Del for speaking, write or phone her at:
Del@delbates.com
You can always find her on her website:
www.Pen4TheLord.com

ENDNOTES

1 Vietnam War Casualties: https://en.wikipedia.org/wiki/Vietnam_War_casualties#Civilian_deaths_in_the_Vietnam_War

2 Terrorism in the United States: https://en.wikipedia.org/wiki/Terrorism_in_the_United_States#2010–present

3 Downs, Frederick Jr, *The Killing Zone: My Life in the Vietnam War*, New York, N.Y., W.W. Norton & Company, Inc., Reissue edition (February 17, 2007).

4 Philippians 3:19; 2 Tim 1:7

5 2 Corinthians 10:5

6 Ephesians 3:20

7 Matthew 14:22-29

8 Savard, Liberty, *Breaking the Power: Of Unmet Needs, Unhealed Hurts, and Unresolved Issues in Your Life*, Plainfield, NJ, Bridge-Logos, 2012, page 50.

9 Psalm 46:10

10 Reference Matthew 4

11 Isaiah 55:9

12 From "The Lord's Prayer," found in Matthew 6 and Luke 11.

13 Reference Exodus 34

14 Reference Matthew 5:45

Printed in the United States
By Bookmasters